THE
EFFECTIVENESS
OF
ANTI-TERRORIST
POLICIES

Christopher Hewitt

UNIVERSITY
PRESS OF
AMERICA

LANHAM • NEW YORK • LONDON

Burgess
HV
6431
.H48
1984

Copy 2

All University Press of America books are produced on acid-free
paper which exceeds the minimum standards set by the National
Historical Publications and Records Commission.

ACKNOWLEDGEMENTS

A number of persons helped me in writing this book. Dr. Papachrysostomou of the Museum of National Struggle, and Peter Loizos of the London School of Economics sent me information on the EOKA campaign. Dr. Robert Clark of George Mason University generously provided material on ETA and the Basques, and helped fill in various lacunae in the published sources. David McKittrick and Conor O'Clery gave me access to the _Irish Times_ death file.

Roger Lewis and Conor O'Clery offered valuable comments on an earlier version of the manuscript. Computer time was provided by the Computer Science Center of the University of Maryland.

The original research, upon which the book is based, was financially supported by the Office of Long Range Assessments and Research, of the Department of State. The views expressed are those of the author, and do not necessarily represent the views of the United States Government or the Department of State.

TABLE OF CONTENTS

LIST OF TABLES

LIST OF OF FIGURES

ix

INTRODUCTION

The purpose of this study is to examine the policies that have been used against urban terrorism, and to evaluate their effectiveness. The analysis is restricted to situations where urban terrorism poses a major threat to society. Most terrorist groups are small; their campaigns short-lived and ineffective.[1] However, such groups are responsible for only a small proportion of terrorist violence. On the other hand a few campaigns have accounted for the great majority of fatalities. During the 1961-70 period, five cases accounted for 80% of all deaths from terrorism, and during the 1966-76 period, two cases for more than 50%.[2] These facts suggest that the most useful research strategy is one that focuses on the major campaigns.

Using such criteria as fatalities, duration, and political or social impact, a list of major terrorist campaigns since the second World War would number about a dozen. This excludes those cases in which urban terrorism was part of a largely rural guerrilla insurgency, and some

---

[1]Ted Gurr "Some Characteristics of Political Terrorism in the 1960s", Stohl (1979). Gurr shows that most groups have less than 50 members and only 10 out of 335 terrorist campaigns lasted more than eighteen months.

[2]See Laqueur, (1977: 213) and Stohl (1979:29).

marginal situations where terrorist activity was a problem but not a major threat to society.[1]

Five cases are selected for detailed examination: the IRA in Northern Ireland (1970-81), ETA in Spain (1975-81), the Red Brigades/Front Line in Italy (1977-81), the Tupamaros in Uruguay (1968-73) and EOKA in Cyprus (1955-58). They were chosen partly because of topical interest - three campaigns were ongoing when research was begun -and partly because exceptionally good data were available. Although the five cases do not constitute a truly random sample, they do include cases from three geographic regions, and examples of both nationalist and revolutionary terrorism. One kind of terrorism, that carried out by groups seeking to defend the status quo, is not examined in this study. The main reason for this omission is that anti-terrorist measures are rarely targeted at this type of violence.

The most original feature of the present study is its use of time-series analysis to measure the effectiveness of different policies. The logic underlying this approach is simple. A successful anti-terrorist policy is one that reduces the amount of terrorist violence. Therefore if the level of terrorist activity is plotted over time, and against some policy indicator, one should be able to decide whether the policy is, or is not, effective. Since different policies have different kinds of impacts, a variety of techniques are used to measure their effectiveness. Some policies are either in operation or not in operation, others vary in intensity from month to month. For the former type of policy a simple before and after comparison is usually

---

[1]In addition to the five cases examined in this study, major urban terrorist campaigns have taken place in Cuba (1953-9), Venezuela (1961-3), Aden (1964-7), Brazil (1966-73), Argentina (1969-75), and Turkey (1973-82). The chronic violence between Israelis and Palestinians could be considered as a series of campaigns, separated by time and place. A more generous definition might include the FLQ in Canada and the Baader-Meinhof gang in West Germany.

sufficient. For the latter type of policy correlation coefficients are calculated. To test
for a delayed rather than an immediate effect,
the violence was lagged for one through six
months. Thus it is possible to see whether policy actions in January affect the violence in the
months February through July. Finally to allow
for the fact that several policies are being
applied simultaneously, multiple regression analysis was employed. Since five terrorist campaigns are examined, cross-national comparisons
can isolate the unique features of each case.

This type of analysis is only possible with
reliable and detailed data on terrorist incidents
and government countermeasures, covering a
lengthly period of time. Fortunately not only do
major terrorist campaigns last a long time, but
they are usually well-recorded in chronologies,
case studies and official statistics.

Selecting a starting date for the analysis is
sometimes difficult. The Cyprus case is easiest
since the campaign opened with a proclamation by
EOKA and a wave of attacks in April 1955. In
Uruguay and Italy, the analysis begins at the
point when the level of terrorism showed a dramatic escalation after several years of intermittent activity. In the case of Spain, there have
been two jumps in terrorist activity, one around
1974-5, the other in 1978. The first date has
been selected because it coincides with the ending of the Franco regime, an obvious watershed in
Spanish society. In Northern Ireland, since most
British Army records begin January 1970, this
date has been chosen as a convenient starting
point.

In Cyprus and Uruguay, almost all terrorist
acts were carried out by a single organization,
EOKA in the former case, the Tupamaros in the
latter. In Northern Ireland, Spain and Italy the
situation is more complex and several groups are
active in each country. In Italy, for example,
as of April 1978, 209 different organizations had
taken credit for terrorist attacks (Ronchey,
1979). This complexity has been reduced by ag-
gregating the activity of terrorist groups within

the same ideological category. Thus no distinction is made between "Provisional" and "Official" IRA actions; both are treated as manifestations of "Republican" terrorism. This can be justified on both theoretical and practical grounds. One would expect theoretically that any policy that reduces terrorism by the Provisionals would also reduce terrorism by the Officials. Furthermore, it is often very difficult in practice to be sure which particular group carried out a given act. In Italy the Red Brigades, Front Line and other Leftist groups use similar tactics against similar targets. Many acts are unclaimed, or are claimed by more than one organization. Some organizations are believed to be "nommes de guerre" of other groups.

The study is focused on macro-policies; micro-policies, such as hostage negotiations or surveillance techniques, will be ignored. The macro-policies examined fall into six categories:

1) Negotiating a ceasefire with the terrorists.

2) Improving economic conditions.

3) Making reforms.

4) The collective punishment of the civilian population.

5) Emergency legislation giving special powers to the authorities and reducing the civil liberties of the general population.

6) Repressive policies involving the use of security forces and the courts.

The book is divided into five sections. Chapter 1 describes, case by case, the social and historical background to the insurgency, the aims, organization, and social composition of the terrorist group and its' internal and external support. Chapter 2 discusses the campaigns and the indicators used to measure terrorist violence. Chapter 3 examines the policies used to reduce terrorism and analyses their effectiveness. Chapter 4 contains a discussion of the findings, which attempts to place them in theoretical context. The data sources and coding procedures are described in an appendix.

Researching an ongoing terrorist campaign is like aiming at a moving target, and any statement made about the situation is in danger of being falsified by events. The reader should bear in mind that the manuscript was first written in 1982, and revised in early 1984. There is usually a lag of at least several months between the collection of statistics and their publication. For Northern Ireland, Spain and Italy the analysis is based on data through December, 1981.

CHAPTER 1

FIVE CASES OF TERRORISM

In this chapter the five cases of terrorism will be considered case by case. For each case the following matters will be discussed: the social and historical background to the insurgency, the aims, organization, numerical strength and social composition of the terrorist group, its popular support and the amount and sources of any external aid received.

EOKA in Cyprus (1955-1959)

In 1955, Cyprus was a British colony and had been so since the island was taken from the Ottoman empire in 1878. The majority of the population (80%) spoke Greek and belonged to the Greek Orthodox church, while 18% were Turkish speaking Moslems. Most villages were either all-Greek or all-Turkish. In the mixed villages and large towns each community lived in its own quarter. The Turkish population was dispersed throughout the island and there was no administrative district in which they constituted a majority.

The Greek Cypriots aspired to "enosis" (union with Greece) and had done so since the early days of British rule. Their sense of Greek identity was encouraged by the schools where Greek history and classics were taught.[1] The church was also a powerful force in maintaining enosist sentiments. Religion and ethnicity were regarded as synonymous. In the first census taken by the British the population was classified Moslem or Orthodox rather than Turkish or Greek. During centuries of foreign rule the Archbishop of the Orthodox church had been the secular as well as spiritual leader of the Greek Cypriot community.

---

[1]Grivas notes that in his village school "the glories of Greek history always took first place" and that his secondary school "like all the others on Cyprus...was staffed with teachers from Greece who brought fresh fervor to our nationalism" (1965:3).

Turkish Cypriots were bitterly opposed to the prospect of Cyprus being united with Greece. As Greek agitation increased, the Turks raised the counter demand of "taksim" (partition) should the British withdraw. Greeks were measurably better off than Turks but this was a result of cultural and educational differences rather than discrimination.[1] For the same reasons, Greeks were slightly overrepresented in the higher levels of the government administration. Social contact between the two communities was slight, with each community patronizing its own institutions, coffee shops and clubs.

In 1931 poor economic conditions, and enosist agitation caused a revolt during which Government House was burnt to the ground. The British responded by deporting two bishops, alleged leaders of the revolt, and by suspending the constitution.

After World War II the enosis issue emerged again. Delegations were sent to London, petitions presented to visiting government officials, and in 1950, in a church sponsored plebiscite 96% of the Greek Cypriots declared themselves in favor of enosis. British proposals for a new constitution were rejected with the slogan "Enosis and nothing but Enosis." In 1952, Archbishop Makarios III began a campaign to gain international support for enosis, visiting London, Athens, Washington, and New York. The Greek government raised the Cyprus question at the United Nations in 1954 and called for a plebiscite.

The origins of EOKA can be traced back to a Cypriot liberation committee set up in Athens by Cypriot emmigres and conservative Greek politicians. In early 1951 Makarios recommended Colonel Grivas to the committee as a military leader should an armed struggle become necessary.

---

[1]Markides (1977:31) claims that Greeks "have always been better off economically than Turks" even under conditions favoring the Turks. He estimates that in 1961, Turkish per capita income was 20% below that of the Greeks.

Grivas was a native-born Cypriot, retired on pension from the Greek army. During World War II he organized a right wing resistance group called Xhi, and gained further experience in irregular warfare fighting the Communists during the Greek civil war. In July 1951, Grivas returned to Cyprus to examine the situation and organize the revolt which began April 1955.

At the start of the revolt EOKA consisted of less than 80 fighters, but this number grew to 273 by February, 1956. At that time EOKA was organized into 47 town groups and 7 groups based in the Troodos mountains. All the groups were small, those in the towns averaging 5 members and those in the mountains somewhat more. In addition there were a number of village groups[1] and sympathizers who acted as couriers, distributed leaflets, and collected information. Grivas exercised an unusual degree of personal control over the organization through an elaborate system of couriers. He picked many of the targets, decided which Greek Cypriots would be executed as "traitors" and for a period even disbursed the petty cash.[2]

Markides (1977:18-20) and Loizos (1975:317-8) provide information as to the demographic and social characteristics of EOKA members. Of those brought to trial for terrorist offenses, such as

---

[1]Loizos (personal communication) suggests that the significance of the village groups has been underestimated in most accounts and that "in most of the Greek villages there was an EOKA unit." Grivas gives a figure of 75 village groups with "approximately 750 men" (1965:67).

[2]"Grivas was obliged to deal with routine matters which fell far outside the scope of a military leader's normal duties. When the pregnant wife of an EOKA prisoner needed to go into a maternity clinic it was the Colonel who granted the request." (Crawshaw, 1978:187).

possession of arms, throwing grenades, or murder, 87% were under 25 years old, and the average age was 21. Those killed in action were somewhat older; 57% were under 25 and the average age was 23. This youthfulness is explained primarily by psychological factors. Grivas himself noted that "among young people one finds audacity, love of taking risks and the thirst for great and difficult achievements" and deliberately recruited such "passionate youth" (1964:14-15). While women played a significant supporting role in the struggle all the active terrorists were men. This fact reflects the traditional nature of Cypriot society. Grivas remarked that "some girls asked me for permission to form a guerilla group but this I did not allow."

Although Grivas and a few other EOKA leaders were from comfortable middle-class backgrounds, the majority of the guerrillas were of working class origin. Those old enough to have left school had jobs "as carpenters, mechanics, or electricians," and an elementary education (Markides 1977:18). Loizos (1978:317-8) found that of 68 EOKA killed in action only two were university graduates and that only 24 had a secondary education. Excluding students the most common occupational categories were farmers (13), craftsmen (12), clerks (7), and laborers (4).

Most commentators agree that the overwhelming majority of Greek Cypriots desired enosis. No evidence suggests that any sizable portion of the population wanted anything else. The only controversy concerns the intensity of their commitment, and the extent to which a desire for enosis involved support for EOKA. There are reasons to believe that many Greek Cypriots were apathetic about enosis and opposed to EOKA. EOKA found it necessary to execute a large number as informers or traitors. Markides (1977:17) notes that no group had any pressing economic reasons to rebel against the British. The peasants and the middle-class were prosperous. Crawshaw gives several examples of the initial reluctance of Cypriots to make sacrifices for EOKA.[1] Bitter antagonism developed between the Cypriot left and the ultra-rightist Grivas.

On the other hand, demonstrations, strikes, and riots were frequent, wide-spread, and well-supported. EOKA sympathizers were found in the police force, the civil service, and among workers on the British bases, which suggests that EOKA could count on a very high degree of spontaneous mass support throughout the Greek community. EOKA could also rely upon the church and the various nationalist organizations to provide an infrastructure throughout the island. The first EOKA cells were recruited from the ranks of two nationalist youth groups, OXEN and PEON. Churches and monasteries were used to store arms and ammunition and as hideouts for the terrorists. The church supplied the terrorists with food and purchased arms and ammunition for them.[2] Some support came from Greece, even from the Greek government. Papagos, the Greek prime minister, knew of Grivas' plans as early as February 1953. Arms were smuggled into Cyprus with the connivance of an Admiral of the Royal Hellenic Navy. Weapons came from Greek army stores. The Greek government kept up diplomatic pressure against Britain at the United Nations, while a torrent of propaganda poured from Athens radio.

----

[1]A priest "charged with finding hideouts for wanted men...suggested that EOKA should rent village houses used by townspeople as summer residences. ...Not even the priests were willing to make undue sacrifices... Before long some of the saboteurs began to demand payment. One man named his price for putting a bomb in a British cargo boat as £100" (Crawshaw, 1978:108,119).

[2]Orthodox clergy even smuggled explosive timers into Cyprus. After a visit abroad, the episcopal staff of the Bishop of Kitium was filled with eight time pencils, while another priest had them sewn into his hat (Foley and Scobie, 1975:58-9).

The Tupamaros of Uruguay (1968-73)

Uruguay in the '60s was not a society where the emergence of a terrorist movement would have been expected. It was one of the most urbanized and economically developed Latin American countries, with a long record of constitutional rule. A welfare state had been created by President Batlle as early as 1915 and the population enjoyed such benefits as a minimum wage, unemployment benefits and old age pensions.

However, the pastoral sector, the basis of the whole economy, had been declining since the late '50s. The result was a low growth rate and a high rate of inflation. Another problem was that the universities turned out an over-supply of liberal arts graduates. While in good times these could be absorbed by expanding the public sector, this was not possible in the depressed conditions of the '60s. Labor militancy and student radicalism both increased dramatically during this period.

In 1959 Raul Sendic, a law student, began to organize the sugar workers of northern Uruguay. His union became increasingly radical, moving from reformist demands for an eight hour day and a minimum wage to a call for the expropriation of uncultivated land. In June 1962 the union organized a march on Montevideo, which ended in violence. Sendic was subsequently arrested and while in jail wrote an article, "Waiting for the Guerrilla," which advocated urban guerrilla warfare. Sometime during the next few months, the Tupamaros were organized under Sendic's leadership. Their first operation was a raid on the Swiss Rifle Club in July 1963.

The Tupamaro ideology was obviously inspired by Castroism. Unlike orthodox Marxist-Leninism which held that the objective conditions for a revolution had to exist prior to revolutionary action, the Tupamaros believed that "revolutionary action in itself...generates revolutionary consciousness, organization, and conditions."[1] Their model for the future was a centrally planned socialist society. Socialism was linked to nationalism through the belief that Uruguay was an exploited dependency of American Imperialism. According to Halperin (1976:53) their Marxist-Leninism was "the doctrine of the neo-Marxist dedependency school that emerged in the late 1960's - a Marxism in essence reduced to an interpretation of the contemporary nonsocialist world as the system of metropolis-satellite or center-periphery relations dominated by the multinational corporations."

The Tupamaros grew from an original nucleus of less than fifty activists in 1965 to about 3,000 in 1970. They were organized into small cells of 2 to 6 members. Cells were linked together to form columns, which operated in particular geographic areas. Some Montevideo columns had a specialized function, such as the medical treatment of wounded guerrillas. Only a minority of the cells were engaged in combat: the rest provided logistic support to the combat cells. Cells and columns had an infrastructure of sympathizers who did not live underground but aided the Tupamaros in various ways. Cell members did not know one anothers' identity and used nicknames and false identity papers. Links between various cells were minimized by the principle of compartmentalization. The group leader of each cell was the only contact between cells and there was no hierarchic structure within columns. Compartmentalization led to a number of problems in coordinating large scale operations (Porzecanski, 1973:36), and in their day to day operations the Tupamaros "appeared to lack a unified command" (Moss, 1972:222). The leadership of the Tupamaros was in the hands

---

[1]This quotation is from "Treinta Preguntas a un Tupamaro" (Thirty Questions to a Tupamaro) based on an interview with a high ranking Tupamaro. The interview is reprinted in several books and an English translation can be found in Kohl and Litt (1974).

of an executive committee which was nominally subject to a national convention made up of represen-
tatives from all guerrilla units. The national
convention, however, seems never to have met after
1970.

Of all the groups considered in this study
the Tupamaros received the least external support
and aid. Porzecanski (1973:23) notes that while
the Tupamaros were interested in developing contacts with revolutionary movements and governments
abroad, they did not begin to do so until 1972,
showing the degree to which they were "politically, ideologically, and militarily independent of
foreign governments." The only international link
reported is that some Tupamaros were sent for
training in Havana after 1968 (Sterling, 1981:
20).[1]

Information on the characteristics of the
Tupamaros, based on those killed and captured, can
be found in Porzecanski (1973), D'Oliveira (1973)
and a 1972 report published by the Interior Ministry. According to Porzecanski, their average age
was 27, and one quarter (25.4%) were women. Occupationally the Tupamaros fell into three groups of
almost equal size; students (29.5%), professional
and technical (32.4%), and workers (32.4%).

The more detailed occupational data presented
by D'Oliveira and the Interior Ministry confirm
the role of students and professionals among the
Tupamaros. However, they show that most of the
"workers" held lower middle class jobs such as
bank clerk or civil servant. Only 5% in
D'Oliveira's sample and 12% in the Ministry Report
were truly working class.

The Tupamaros had a number of well-placed
sympathizers in the police, the military, the
civil service, and the banks, all of whom provided
them with vital information. A network of support

---

[1]"No evidence has been found that the Tupamaros ever received either money or arms from other
countries or from social movements abroad" Porzecanski (1973:41).

groups (Comites de Apoyo a los Tupamaros) was organized in the trade unions and among high school
and college students. The Tupamaros themselves
saw students as the group that supported them the
most strongly. Their relationship with the Uruguayan Communist Party and other left wing parties
was cordial, but ambivalent, since the Tupamaros
believed that armed struggle was the only way to
win power. However, the Tupamaros willingly par-
ticipated in the Frente Amplio, an electoral
alliance of left wing groups, as a means of mobil-
izing the masses. The Frente Amplio got 19% of
the vote in the 1971 election--one measure of public support for the Tupamaros.[1] Another measure
is a public opinion poll which asked whether the
Tupamaros were motivated by a "concern for social
justice." In mid 1971 59% of the population believed they were, but this figure dropped to 4% by
the end of 1972. Not only was there public sympathy for the Tupamaros, but also the government's
image was tarnished by several well-publicized examples of corruption. The result was that the
contest between government and Tupamaros resembled
"a football match in which the people felt themselves to be spectators" (Moss 1972:233).

Northern Ireland and the IRA (1970 -   )

Politically, Northern Ireland belongs to the
United Kingdom; geographically, it is part of Ireland. In the seventeenth century, Scottish and
English Protestants were settled in Northern Ireland, dispossessing the Gaelic population. The
current division between Protestants and Catholics
results from that historical act. The Protestants
are, in general, descendants of the settlers,
while most of the native Irish remained Catholic.

Religious identity provides (and has histor-
ically provided) the basis for communal identity.

---

[1]The Frente Amplio (Broad Front) was composed
of fourteen left-wing groups including the March
26 Movement, a group closely identified with the
Tupamaros. The Front drew disproportionate support from the upper class (McDonald, 1972).

Both communities have distinctive traditions, and most organizations are aligned with one community or the other. Even prior to the current conflict there was a high degree of voluntary segregation between the two communities.

These communal identities are significant politically. When Irish Nationalism emerged as a serious force in the nineteenth century, it drew mass support only from the Catholic population. The Protestants, in contrast, organized against home rule and for remaining a part of the United Kingdom.

Militant Irish Nationalists rebelled against the British in 1916. Their campaign was effective in the twenty six Catholic counties, but had little impact in the six Northern counties where Protestants predominated. Eventually, in 1921 Ireland was partitioned, the twenty six Catholic counties becoming the Irish Free State while the other six remained part of the United Kingdom. Within Northern Ireland, Protestants outnumbered Catholics about two to one, a figure which remained remarkably constant throughout the period since the higher Catholic birthrate was exactly matched by a higher rate of emigration.[1]

The sectarian geography of Northern Ireland is important because it largely explains the geographical distribution of violence. The practicality of certain policies, such as repartition or administrative decentralization, is limited by the fact that Catholics are a numerical majority in only a few areas. There are three main regions, an eastern heavily-Protestant zone, a western zone in which the two groups are evenly-balanced and a broken strip of land along the border where Catholics are in a clear majority. In the two

---

[1]In 1961 there were 929,000 Protestants and 497,000 Catholics. The percentage of Catholics was 34.9% in 1961 and 34.2% in 1911. In 1971 and 1981, many people refused to identify themselves by religion. The declining rate of emigration has probably increased the proportion of Catholics since 1961.

largest towns, Belfast and Londonderry, the communities are residentially segregated. In Belfast, Catholics are the minority (27%) while in Londonderry they form the majority (67%).

Northern Irish politics traditionally revolved around "the national question" with Protestants overwhelmingly supporting the British link and a plurality of Catholics favoring a United Ireland. However, a sizable minority of Catholics does accept the existing constitutional situation.[1] The position of the Catholic minority within Northern Ireland was until recently a secondary issue. Catholics claimed that they were treated as second-class citizens, and discriminated against in various ways.[2]

In the early 1960s, the Northern Irish Civil Rights Association (NICRA) organized a series of protests against discrimination. Many Protestants saw these demonstrations as Republican-inspired attacks on the state, and clashes between Catholic and Protestant crowds took place. As communal violence escalated, the U.K. government intervened, sending in the army in July 1969 and taking over the administration of the province in March 1972.

The IRA, one of the oldest terrorist groups in the world, can be traced back, ideologically and organizationally, to the mid-nineteenth century. During the 1916-21 struggle for Irish independence, the IRA were the backbone of the rebel forces. When the Anglo-Irish Treaty was signed, a civil war broke out in Southern Ireland between the pro-Treaty forces and the anti-Treaty forces

---

[1]In 1968 33% of the Catholics approved of the constitutional position of Northern Ireland (Rose 1971:189) and in the most recent poll (Sunday Times, 6/28/81) 39% favored complete integration with Great Britain.

[2]For a discussion of the situation of the Catholics prior to the present troubles see Rose (1971) and Hewitt (1981).

(i.e. the IRA). Although militarily defeated, the IRA survived as the embodiment of the most intransigeant form of Irish Nationalism. Their goal was to end partition and create a "Thirty Two County Republic," not only driving out the British forces "occupying" the Six Countries but also toppling the treacherous "Twenty-six County" government.

Intermittent terrorist attacks were made against both English and Northern Irish targets. After the failure of the 1956-62 campaign, the IRA leadership embraced Marxism, and abandoned the physical force strategy. The result was that when communal rioting broke out in 1969 the IRA could not protect the Catholic community. This in turn led to a split between the "Officials" and the "Provisionals." The former group is Marxist, the latter are traditional Nationalists who favor military rather than political action. The Provisionals are the major terrorist organization on the Republican side, but some attacks have been carried out by the Officials or by the Irish National Liberation Army.[1]

The IRA was, in the past, organized in pseudo-military fashion with battalions, companies and a clearly defined hierarchy of officers, including Commanding Officers, Quartermasters and Information Officers. The battalions are territorially organized with a battalion based in each of the centers of Catholic population. Each company is composed of local "volunteers" who operate in their home district. This military-style organization was extremely vulnerable to penetration and around 1977 was replaced by a system of small cells in which members had little knowledge of their superiors.[2] The IRA reached a maximum strength of 2,000 in 1972, but now numbers about 500 (Holland, 1981:145).

---

[1] The Irish National Liberation Army is the military wing of the Irish Republican Socialist Party, a breakaway faction of the Officials.

[2] According to Boyle et al (1980:18) "the extent of this change has probably been exaggerated" and the traditional structure still persists.

Information is available on the characteristics of IRA volunteers killed in action or convicted of terrorist offences. Of those killed in action the average age was 20; 73% were under 25. The ages ranged from 14 to 47; the most common age 17 years. Of those convicted in 1979 more than half (53%) were under 21 and another fifth were aged between 21 and 25. In 1975 the group was even younger with 70% under 21 and 13% aged between 21 and 25.

Only a handful were women, reflecting the traditional nature of Irish society. Fighting is a male activity and women are only expected to play a supporting role in the struggle. Furthermore, working class Catholics marry young, get pregnant quickly, and have large families. It is therefore unlikely that Catholic women have much time to spare for terrorist activities.

The socioeconomic background of the IRA killed in action is lower working class. The most common job listed is unskilled laborer. Often they are unemployed. In Belfast the IRA volunteers come from the most deprived areas of the city. Seventeen wards in Belfast are classified as "areas of special need" in terms of housing, health and poverty; 89% of the dead IRA men were from these wards. The three Belfast wards with the highest male unemployment rates, Whiterock (49%), New Lodge (41%), and Clonard (36%) account for more than half of the fatalities.[1] According to an analysis of those arrested for terrorist offenses in early 1975, 75% had working class occupations, and 34% were unemployed at the time of arrest. (Fortnight, May 7, 1976)

---

[1]The analysis of the characteristics of the IRA is based on Boyle et al (1980) and on my own research into IRA fatalities. The obituaries in the Irish News allow a reconstruction of family size and fertility. Those aged 20, and under were single, those over 20 were married. The husbands' mean age was 22 when his first child was born, 25 when his second child was born. By age 35 the typical volunteer had five children. For the most recent British Army assessment of the IRA (the Glover Report) see Holland (1981:147).

The degree of support for the Provisional IRA within the Catholic community is variously estimated and has also fluctuated over time. British army sources conceded in August 1971 that one quarter of the Catholics in Belfast and Londonderry were helping the IRA and another half were sympathizers. Clutterbuck (1980:72) suggests that in 1972 the Catholic population in Belfast, Londonderry and the border areas of South Armagh was "solidly behind them." Most estimates agree that support fell even in the hard core areas to "less than one third" by 1975, and to between one quarter and a third in 1978.

The Hunger Strike by convicted IRA terrorists clearly increased Catholic support for the IRA. A by-election for the constituency of Fermanagh and South Tyrone was won by one of the hunger strikers in April 1981. In October 1982, Provisional Sinn Fein contested elections to the Northern Irish Assembly for the first time, and won 64,000 votes. In the United Kingdom general elections of June 1983, Sinn Fein obtained 103,000 votes, compared to 137,000 going to the other Catholic party, the Social Democratic and Labour Party.

Support for the IRA depends on a number of factors. A majority of Catholics share their aims even if they disapprove of their methods. IRA violence itself is legitimated by the rebel tradition in Irish history. Terrorist operations are carried out by local youths on targets close to their homes. This insures that they will be known to the population of the local area as neighbors, friends, or relatives and will be protected and sheltered because of such local links.[1]

---

[1]A comparison of home address and place killed for Belfast IRA volunteers "killed in action" shows that the average distance between the two was just over a half a mile. When an IRA volunteer is killed in action, the Catholic paper, Irish News, usually contains dozens of obituary notices placed by relatives, friends, workmates and neighbors. By looking at their addresses it can be seen that IRA volunteers swim in a sea of relatives and friends.

This local support is further increased by two factors. In the Catholic ghettos of Belfast the IRA functions as a defense force, patrolling its borders and protecting the inhabitants from Protestant assassins or rioters. Those areas of Belfast attacked by Protestant rioters in 1968 continue to be IRA strongholds.[1] A vicious cycle also maintains sympathy for the IRA. IRA attacks on the British Army result in Army searches; in turn leading to further alienation of the public, to more IRA attacks and so on.

External aid to the IRA has come from several sources. In the latter part of 1969 the IRA asked for and received both guns and money from the Dublin government. Some of this aid was diverted from official government funds voted by the Dail (the Irish Legislature) for humanitarian relief to the North. One steady source of aid has been the Irish-American community, which has contributed large sums to NORAID, an organization which supposedly provides aid to civilian victims of the conflict. It is generally accepted that NORAID money has been diverted to buy guns.[2]

---

[1] In the communal rioting of August 1969, Protestants burnt out Bombay Street. One British Army officer comments that the "Burning of Bombay Street was the oft-repeated and most regarded underlying justification for the IRA's claim to be needed as the only defense force that the Catholics of Belfast could rely on in dire emergency to protect their lives and homes. The bulk of the Catholic population accepted this claim and...were not prepared to cooperate with the forces of the Crown to destroy the IRA, just in case another 'Bombay Street' situation might arise, with no one but the IRA to keep the murdering Protestant mob away from them" (Evelegh, 1978:7).

[2] From July 1974 to July 1977, NORAID sent $812,530 to Northern Ireland. Most British soldiers have been killed by the U.S.-made M16. In 1982, three NORAID members, including Michael Flannery, the founder of the organization, were charged with conspiracy to receive and possess automatic weapons, and to export weapons without a license. Their trial is described in "Terror in Northern Ireland: The American Connection," Readers Digest, April 1983.

The IRA has received an increasing degree of assistance from other terrorist groups and from the Soviet bloc countries.[1] In late 1971 the first shipment of Czech arms to the IRA was intercepted in the Netherlands. A handful of IRA volunteers have been trained in PLO camps in Lebanon and South Yemen. Some tenuous connections have been developed with the German RAF, the Italian Red Brigades and the Basque ETA.

The Basques and E.T.A. (1975-   )

The Basques speak a language unrelated to any other in the world and their historical origins are disputed. The Basque homeland straddles the Western Pyrenees with about 200,000 Basques living in France, and the remainder in Spain. The Basque region of Spain is composed of four provinces inhabited by just over 2.3m people. Immigration into the Basque provinces from other parts of Spain has been heavy and ethnic Basques constitute only about 60% of the population. The proportion of Basque-speakers is considerably less, just under 20%.[2]

Basque ethnicity is interesting in that a division between Basque and non-Basque is difficult to make with any precision. Possibly related to this is the fact that Basques and non-Basques

---

[1] Russian-made RPG-7 Rocket launchers were used by the IRA in November 1972. Two Soviet diplomats were expelled from the Irish Republic for meeting with IRA leaders in 1983. It was claimed that the Soviets were trading arms for military information. (New York Times, 9/26/83).

[2] According to Nunez-Astrain, 51% had parents both of whom had identifiable Basque surnames, while 8% had one parent with a Basque surname (1977:168). For an excellent discussion of the Basque situation see Clark (1979).

do not form two separate social communities.
There is no residential segregation and neither
social activities nor social institutions are
linked to ethnicity.[1]

The last independent united Basque state was
the Kingdom of Navarra which lasted until 1035.
Thereafter the Basque area south of the Pyrenees
gradually came under the control of the Spanish
monarchy. However, each of the Basque provinces
retained a high degree of autonomy and its own
laws ("fueros"). In the nineteenth century, when
a centralized Spanish state began to emerge, the
Basque coastal provinces became the most industri-
alized region of Spain.

Basque nationalism dates from the latter part
of the nineteenth century, the Basque Nationalist
Party (PNV) having been founded in 1895 by Sabino
de Arana. The Nationalist movement struggled to
revive the Basque language which it saw as central
to Basque identity. The movement was strongly
Catholic, drew its initial support from the petit
bourgeoisie and favored a non-violent parliamentary strategy.

The PNV remained the main vehicle of Basque
nationalism throughout the military dictatorship
of Primo de Rivera, the second Republic and the
Civil War. During the Civil War the PNV sided
with the Republic and in return the provinces of
Guipuzcoa, and Vizcaya were granted autonomy.
The autonomous government had a brief existence
from October 1936 until June 1937 when Franco's
forces overran the territory.

---

[1]Based on personal communication from Professor Clark, George Mason University. Unlike
Northern Ireland there is only a slight relationship between ethnicity and class, and ethnic Basques have an income 10% higher than non-Basques
(Nunez-Astrain, 1977:168-173).

Basque nationalism was savagely repressed under Franco but a resistance movement gradually developed. In the 1950s younger and more radical Basques became increasingly dissatisfied with the PNV leadership, and formed Euzkadi ta Askatasuna (ETA) in 1959. A bitter ideological dispute within ETA went on for several years and led to a number of splits within the movement.[1] The main issues concerned cooperation with the Spanish left and the role of violence in revolutionary war. At present three groups can be identified, all of which consider themselves Marxists engaged in a national liberation struggle. The most important organization is ETA-militar (ETA-m) which advocates armed struggle as the primary strategy, and has been responsible for most deaths in the conflict. ETA-politico-militar (ETA-pm) favors a combined military and political strategy and its violence has been more restrained than that of ETA-m. A third group, much smaller than the other two but the most fanatical, is called Comandos Autonomos.

ETA has an elaborate organizational structure. An executive committee controls day-to-day activities but is responsible to an annual assembly. The organization is divided into four fronts according to function; worker organization, cultural, political and military. The membership is divided into three categories, "liberados," "legales," and "apoyos." The first category, who work for the organization full-time and are paid a small salary carry out the actual attacks. The legales, who continue to hold regular jobs, gather intelligence and act as couriers. The apoyos supply shelter and other kinds of support to the active members. The basic unit is the "comando," a small cell of three to five persons. The number of active members, liberados plus legales, has fluctuated over time. Clark (1981) estimates that there have been two peaks, in 1968 when the membership total was about 600, and in 1979 when it may have reached 700.

---

[1]The various factions are sometimes labeled in terms of the assemblies during which the splits occurred. Thus ETA militar is sometimes referred to as ETA 5, and ETA politico-militar as ETA 6.

The process of becoming an ETA member is a gradual one. The potential recruit becomes more and more involved in the organization as he participates in increasingly dangerous operations. Clark's analysis shows the typical "etarra" to be male (91%) and in his mid' twenties (mean age is 25 years). Occupationally the etarras are fairly representative of the general Basque population, except that the middle class is overrepresented and there are few farmers and few unemployed. One very interesting fact about the current generation of etarras is that a high proportion (22%) are not ethnic Basques or are of mixed Spanish and Basque descent (38%).

According to most sources, support for ETA was strong until recently. Bell described ETA as "not simply tolerated but protected" (1978:191). A 1978 survey found that at least a third of the Basque population were favorable to ETA. The consensus holds that support has declined since the granting of autonomy. In February 1981, extensive demonstrations took place in the Basque provinces against ETA terrorism (Washington Star, 2/10/81).

In the 1979 election the three Basque nationalist parties (PNV, HB, and EE) together received 40-50% of the votes cast. Herri Batasuna (HB), the political arm of ETA, received 13% of the vote in the parliamentary elections and 15% in the municipal elections. However, in the February 1984 elections for the regional assembly, the party's share of the vote declined slightly. Clark notes that the geographical distribution of ETA violence corresponds very closely to the distribution of support for HB and EE, being concentrated in a few towns in Vizcaya and Guipuzcoa.

Basque nationalists, unlike Greek Cypriots and Northern Irish Catholics, cannot count on the support of a friendly homeland. However, the Basque area of France provides sanctuary for etarras on the run from the Spanish police, while French Basques supply money and weapons. Since October 1972, however, the French government has officially banned ETA from operating in France.

ETA is reported to have received aid and guerrilla training from Cuba, Algeria, the Soviet Union and Libya. They may have some links with the IRA, as well as contacts with Breton, Palestinian and Italian terrorists. The IRA connection dates back to 1971 when the two organizations traded revolvers for explosives training. Since then they have engaged in joint gun-running operations. The IRA allegedly supplied the explosives for the assassination of Carrero Blanco.

Revolutionary-Leftists in Italy (1977-   )

The current wave of Italian terrorism began in late 1969. Initially it was the extreme right that was responsible for most terrorist acts and for most terrorist related deaths. Sometime in the mid 1970's the situation changed in several ways.[1] The number of terrorist incidents increased, there were more assassinations, kidnappings, and shootings. Most important, violence by the extreme right declined and violence by the extreme left increased. It is this second wave of revolutionary leftist terrorism that will be examined.

Several factors are suggested as explaining or contributing to the emergence of leftist terrorism at this time. Italy had experienced an economic boom through the '50's and early '60's during which the country had been transformed into a modern industrial society. Massive population movements had taken place from the South to the North and from country to city. However, in the mid '60's the rate of economic growth declined, and worker unrest surfaced in 1969.

---

[1]Ronchey (1979) dates the current phase from 1976 and suggests a distinction between Rightist terrorism using bombs and Leftist terrorism using revolvers and machine guns. According to Furlong "1974 is particularly apt as the dividing-point. It saw the maturity of the strategy of the BR into the objective of striking at the heart of the state...the demotion of the efforts of the neo-fascists...and...the emergence of a variety of left-wing groups" (in Lodge, 1981).

Students as well as workers were affected by the economic situation. The rapid expansion of higher education from the mid '60's onwards meant that a university degree was no longer an automatic passport to a middle class occupation. A weak economy exacerbated this problem.

Economic change was accompanied by social changes so extreme as to constitute a cultural revolution. Traditional family discipline was weakened, academic structures first in the colleges and then in the high schools were challenged From 1969 to 1975 the government enacted legislation that liberalized criminal penalties and procedures. According to Pisano (1979:40) "the birth of contemporary Italian terrorism took place in this climate of ... government weakness and permissiveness."

The "opening to the Left" by the Christian democrats and the willingness of the Communist party (PCI) to adopt a moderate non-revolutionary stance meant that militant revolutionaries had to find a new strategy. As the PCI moved toward the center, it lost control of the extreme left. The result was the emergence of groups such as Worker Power, Continuous Struggle and Proletarian Left, and a polemic over the issue of "armed struggle." From such groups and out of this debate, emerged the Red Brigades, Front Line, Armed Proletarian Nucleii (NAP) and other revolutionary terrorist organizations.

Many Italians, not only those on the extreme left, feared that a rightist coup was imminent. Consequently some felt that the way to preempt this threat was to establish clandestine organizations which could carry out armed resistance if necessary.[1]

---

[1]While generally agreeing on the causes Pisano (1979), Ronchey (1979) and Silj (1979) differ as to their significance. Silj emphasizes the genuine dangers of a Rightist coup, while Pisano dismisses such fears as "paranoid."

Well over one hundred terrorist groups belonging to the extreme left have been identified. However most groups have been responsible for only a few attacks. Also, it is suspected that some groups use different names both to confuse the authorities and to create the impression of a wide-spread revolutionary movement.

The three main groups are the Red Brigades, the Front Line and Armed Proletarian Nucleii. The Red Brigades founded by Renato Curcio, developed out of the Proletarian Left and began operating in 1971. The Armed Proletarian Nucleii (NAP) emerged in the aftermath of the prison riots of 1969-1974, linking together radicalized criminals and dissident members of the Continuing Struggle organization. Front Line first became active in 1976. There has been coordination between the Red Brigades and the NAP and between the Red Brigades and the Front Line. Indeed by 1978 the NAP had apparently been absorbed by the Red Brigades.

The ideology of the Italian leftist groups is variously characterized as Maoist, New Leftist, or Anarchist. They draw inspiration from several sources; from Leninism the idea of a vanguard group which would raise the revolutionary consciousness of the proletariat, and from Maoism a hostility towards the revisionism of the PCI. They were communists who still believed, unlike the PCI, that a communist revolution was a realistic possibility in the near future.[1] Other influences were the Tupamaros and - particularly for the NAP - the writings of the American Black prisoners movement.[2]

------

[1]This is suggested by their use of the term "Berlinguer's party" to describe the PCI, and by the choice of titles such as "Fighting Communists," "Revolutionary Communist Vanguard" or "Revolutionary Communists" for their own groups.

[2]One of the earliest NAP cells was called the Jackson Collective and one NAP militant was buried with a copy of George Jackson's book Blood in My Eye (Silj, 1979:130-1).

The Red Brigades are organized like a pyramid. At the lowest level are cells with four to five members. Two non-communicating but paired cells make up a brigade and the brigades in turn are grouped into columns. The first three columns were in the "Industrial Triangle," Genoa, Milan, and Turin. By 1978 there was a fourth column in Rome and possibly one in Naples. At the top of the Red Brigades there is a strategic command, made up of column commanders concerned with policy and operational strategy. Each level is "sealed" by the fact that a given unit is headed by one person who acts as a filter to the higher levels. The NAP was not so well organized, members were recruited indiscriminately and the various operational units were not compartmentalized (Pisano, 1979:81). The Front line is made up of "fire groups" instead of columns; leadership is exercised on a situational basis, operation by operation, and each fire group operates in a different city from where its members live (Pisano, 1979:86).

Most sources agree that circa 1978 the Red Brigades had about 700 to 800 members, which suggests that all the leftist groups together numbered about 1,500-2,000. Silj estimated that there were at least 1,000 terorists living underground and another 3-8,000 part-time guerrillas (Silj, 1979: xix). Since then, however, their strength has probably declined significantly. Hundreds of Front Line terrorists were arrested in 1980 and scores of Red Brigades members after the Dozier kidnapping.

According to Sterling (1981:216) the active terrorists are supported by a well organized network of supporters, the "Autonomous Area," involving "as many as 200,000" radicals. Others give a lower figure. Time (5/1/78:29) suggests 10,000 sympathizers, and Silj (1979:xvi) says that "10,000 would seem to represent a reasonable estimate...of the numerical strength of Autonomia." The degree of popular sympathy for the terrorists is higher than one might expect. According to a poll in L'Espresso (1/10/1982) almost a third of the population agree that the Red Brigades are pursuing "a just end with the wrong means" and one in ten that they are "fighting for a better society." Among the young, the figures were even higher. One distinctive feature of Italian terrorism is its links to criminal groups, such as the Mafia. The Mafia and Red Brigades have carried out at least some robberies and kidnappings as joint ventures, splitting the proceeds 50-50. The Italian terrorists are alleged to be an important component of the international network of terrorist groups (Sterling, 1981:219-220) and there is some evidence that they received training in and arms from Czecheslovakia.[1]

Only fragmentary information exists on the characteristics of Italian terrorists, and different organizations appear to recruit from different strata. Most of the historic nucleus of the Red Brigaded had been captured or killed by the end of 1977. Of this group, 95% were men and the median age was 27. The socioeconomic background of the terrorists is quite varied. Furlong (in Lodge, 1981:76) says that the Red Brigades recruit mainly "from the universities, among the urban unemployed, and in the prisons." This is confirmed by a reanalysis of the biographical data given in Pisano (1979) and Silj (1979). Of 36 terrorists 47% were manual workers, 31% were students and 18% had a criminal background.[2] Galleni's list of the occupations of 37 terrorists killed in action (1981:76) shows 11 students, 7 workers, 6 unemployed and the remainder mostly white collar jobs such as teacher or clerk. However, given that most terrorists are young, and

---

[1]The most recent evidence of their international connections was provided by two Red Brigades members, turned states evidence, who testified that they had received weapons from the Palestinians, New York Times (11/9/81).

[2]Professor Salierno of Padova claims that in 1981 the Red Brigades recruited an even higher proportion of working class members, which he attributes to the growth in unemployment, Sunday Times (1/3/82).

that for many being a terrorist is their primary
role, such occupational data must be interpreted
with caution. More important than their occupational background is their political history.
Most of the known Italian terrorists have at one
time or another belonged to the PCI, to its youth
oranization or to one or more of the extra parliamentary leftist groups (Pisano, 1979:67).

The inability of the Red Brigades to provoke
a revolution in Italy led to a fierce internal
debate from which two factions emerged, the
"Movimentalists" and the "Militarists." The
Movimentalists see the armed struggle as a spontaneous expression of the class struggle directly
linked to mass needs and tensions. By contrast
the Militarists view themselves as a vanguard,
which is autonomous from the working class.
Leaders of the Movimentalist faction linked Red
Brigade actions to popular grievances by demand-
ing, for example, that homeless Neapolitans be
housed in exchange for the return of kidnap victim
Cirillo. The kidnapping of General Dozier in December 1981 was carried out by Senzani, one of the
leaders of the Militarist faction. The more ad-
venturous strategy of the Militarist faction pro-
voked a massive police crackdown in the aftermath
of the Dozier kidnapping, with large numbers of
terrorists being captured. Since 1982 there has
been only intermittent activity by the Red Brigades and other leftist groups. Prime Minister
Craxi in February 1984 told the Italian Parliament
that terrorism had been "reduced to a few pockets
of resistance."

Summary

There are both similarities and differences among the cases just described. Each of the main terrorist groups had a sizable membership of several hundreds when at maximum strength. In this respect they are, as noted earlier, unusual since most terrorist groups are much smaller. In all five cases, the typical terrorist was a male in his twenties. This feature of terrorism is similar to what is found with street crime, rioting and other types of violence, and is presumably explained by cultural and biological factors.[1]

The Red Brigades, and Tupamaros are examples of revolutionary terrorism, the IRA, EOKA and ETA examples of nationalist terrorism. The goal of the first type is a socialist revolution within the existing nation-state, while the second type seeks national self-determination on the basis of ethnic identity.

Nationalist and Revolutionary terrorists have very different social characteristics. The three nationalist groups approximate a cross-section of the ethnic community from which they are recruited. Paradoxically, in the case of revolutionary terrorist groups, who claim to be acting for the people, the working class is underrepresented, and a disproportionate number of their members are students or from upper-middle class occupations.

The degree of support for nationalist terrorists is much greater than that for the Tupamaros or Red Brigades. As the Maoist phrase describes it they "swim like fish in a sea of popular support." A majority of Greek Cypriots, Northern

---

[1]Even among revolutionary groups which thoretically support sexual equality, women constitute a distinct minority, albeit larger than among nationalist terrorists.

Irish Catholics and Basques have given at least passive support to "their" terrorists. This support may decline temporarily but usually remains at a high level or even increases, during the campaign. In contrast, popular support for the Tupamaros and Red Brigades is more restricted, providing not a sea but a few puddles. The next chapter will examine the differences between nationalist and revolutionary terrorist campaigns.

CHAPTER 2

MEASURING TERRORISM

In constructing measures of terrorist activity it is desirable to keep in mind the nature of the campaign as well as the data that are available. The three campaigns waged by nationalist groups (EOKA, IRA and ETA) have certain obvious similarities; all three have generated a high number of fatalities and their main targets have been the military and the police. In Cyprus there were 1,144 attacks on the British Army during the emergency, and in Northern Ireland 15,146 incidents in which the security forces were fired upon Campaign characteristics are related to nationalist perceptions of their situation. They see their territory as occupied by foreigners and their strategy is to raise the cost of this occupation until the foreigners withdraw. Soldiers and policemen are not only symbols of foreign domination, they are also easy targets and killing them is a simple way of raising costs to the occupying power. One writer, closely associated with the Provisional IRA leadership, describes well the tactical advantage of the terrorists over the security forces.

"The British soldiers were very vulnerable, as are any uniformed force in a guerrilla war. Our Volunteers could recognize them; whereas they could never be sure who amongst the civilians around them was friend, who enemy... But in areas like Andersonstown, they were very clear targets, a sniper could fire a single shot with a modern weapon like an SLR or an M1 carbine from a bedroom window a hundred yards away or more and then take cover and withdraw, or even stand up above a garden wall and pick off the last man in a patrol. A Volunteer once told me it was "like aiming at the moving ducks in a fairground shooting gallery" (Maguire, 1973:75).

Most security force deaths resulted from sniping, explosions or assassinations of off-duty and unarmed personnel. Only very rarely can encounters between the security forces and the terrorists be properly described as battles. As table 1 shows, members of the security force make up the largest single category of terrorist victims in all three cases.[1]

TABLE 1   FATALITIES CAUSED BY NATIONALIST TERRORISTS

	By EOKA	By IRA	By ETA
Total Killings	394	1029	280
1000 population	.69	.69	.11
Victim Type(%)			
Security Forces	40	55	55
Spies and informers	36	2	8
Government officials and politicians	8	1	10
Other civilians selected for personal characteristics	3	7	7
Civilians victims selected on basis of ethnic identity, or accidental victims	13	35	20

Some civilians are murdered because, as government officials or politicians, they are associated with the regime. Other victims deliberately selected by the terrorists include informers and people associated with another terrorist faction. EOKA's campaign was unusual in that the number of Greek Cypriots executed as informers almost equaled the number of security forces killed by EOKA.

---

[1]Figures for ETA and IRA are up to the end of 1980. There is no evidence that the distribution has changed since that date.

The remaining civilian deaths are of relevance in evaluating the claim by terrorist groups to be "guerrillas" or "partisans." Such a claim requires that they do not deliberately kill innocent non-combatants and try to minimize accidental deaths. According to this criterion, ETA has the best claim to guerrilla status. EOKA killed very few people accidentally but deliberately murdered a significant number of British civilians who were clearly non-combatants.[1] Republican terrorists in Northern Ireland have carried out a number of sectarian killings; the most recent example being the November 1983 incident in which a Protestant Church congregation in the village of Darkley was attacked by INLA, and three people murdered. More importantly large numbers of civilians have died as a result of explosions set by the Provisional IRA. The use of explosives by the IRA differs from that of EOKA or ETA in that most of their targets are non- military. By bombing shops, restaurants, offices, etc. without adequate warning, a high civilian fatality rate is almost unavoidable.[2] Given the high fatality rate in nationalist campaigns it seems appropriate to use deaths as one measure of terrorist activity. In addition for Northern Ireland, statistics on explosions and attacks against the security forces are available.

The campaigns of the Tupamaros and the Italian Leftists differ from those of nationalist groups in two ways. First, far fewer people were killed; 84 in Italy, only 26 in Uruguay. The Tupamaros' operations are given below in Table 2, and it is clear most were not intended to result

---

[1]In one notorious incident two British women were shot in the back while shopping with their children (Foley and Scobie, 1975:147) Crawshaw (1978:205) charges that many times EOKA, if unable to kill informers, executed their relatives.

[2]In the great majority of cases, the IRA does give sufficient notice for buildings to be evacuated. Apologists for the IRA claim that a tardy response by the authorities is the cause of most bombing deaths.

in death or physical injury. The Red Brigades,
and other Italian groups do attack individuals but
the goal is usually to wound rather than to kill;
for example, the practice of shooting people in
the leg.

TABLE 2   TUPAMARO ACTIONS BY TYPE (%)

Robberies for money	30.3
Robberies for weapons	9.2
Sabotage	30.3
Propaganda	10.5
Kidnappings	2.1
Attacks on Police/Army	10.9
Attacks on civilians	3.8
Other Actions	2.9
	100.0

The second difference lies in the targets.
For leftists, unlike nationalists, the police and
military are not initially the main targets. Instead they attack businessmen, judges, conservative politicians and other groups linked to the
establishment (see Table 3). The security forces
are killed because they get in the way of the terrorists attacking other targets, or because

they are specifically engaged in antiterrorist activities.[1]

TABLE 3 VICTIMS OF LEFTIST TERRORISM IN ITALY (%)
(1977-81)

Corporate executives	31.3
Police	30.9
Judges and Lawyers	6.4
Right-wing Politicians	12.1
Left-wing politicians	2.6
Journalists, Professors, etc.	6.1
No political/establishment links or no information	10.6
	100.0

Note: Total number of victims (killed, wounded or kidnapped) was 265.

---

[1]The selectivity of the Tupamaros and of the Red Brigades is often noted. According to Porzecanski (1973:48) "Tupamaro tactics...were undertaken with great marksmanship, avoided the use of indiscriminate violence and concentrated on delivering one individual blow after another." Moss (1972:230) says the Tupamaros "remained very selective in their use of terror...Until late in 1969, the guerrillas avoided bloodshed, and their only victims were gunned down when police closed in and forced them to fight a street battle." An Italian official notes "Since the Red Brigades normally claim credit for their violent acts with special messages, the singling out of the victim and the personalization of the attack are very important for this group; it is based on its ability to select appropriate victims that the group measures its operational efficiency and the psychological and political efficiency of its attack" (Anonymous, 1978:162).

While all the terrorist campaigns, whether nationalist or leftist, were primarily directed at domestic targets, there was a tendency for the leftist groups to define their enemies in more international terms. In Uruguay, 16% of the bombings and robberies were directed against diplomatic facilities or foreign businesses. The United States was a particular target with 33 attacks on American businesses and 4 bombings of American Embassy property. Ten percent of the attacks on persons were against foreigners, including the kidnapping of the British consul, the Brazilian consul, an Argentinian businessman, and an American agricultural expert. The most notorious incident was the kidnapping and killing of Dan Mitrione, a USAID official. In Italy, sources record 14 bombings of American businesses and diplomatic facilities, and 4 attacks on other foreign-owned property. This is in addition to 147 attacks on German establishments in 1977 (Pisano, 1979:894). Prior to the kidnapping of General Dozier in December, 1981 only Italians were victims, but two shootings were of Italian exceecutives of foreign corporations (Chemical Bank of New York and the Swiss-owned Icmesa Chemical Company).

The attractiveness of foreign targets to the Tupamaros and the Red Brigade is explained by ideological considerations. The Tupamaros saw Latin America as dominated by Western capitalism, and to the Red Brigades, Italy was part of an "Imperialist State of the Multinationals" (Pisano, 1979:70). Revolutionary leftists are likely to see their campaign as part of a global struggle, and to act in solidarity with revolutionary groups in other countries. Hence the wave of attacks on West German targets in Italy, following the Mogadiscu and Stammheim affairs.

Nationalist terrorists are more parochial than leftists and less likely to attack foreign targets. The handful of cases in which foreigners were victims of EOKA, IRA or ETA terrorism were usually accidents. In Cyprus, in three separate incidents one American was killed and seven wounded. After an explosion which killed the U.S. vice consul and injured three other Americans, Grivas apologized publicly and pointed out that it was difficult to distinguish Americans from British

(Grivas, 1964:72-3). In Northern Ireland, seven foreigners have died as a result of terrorist violence; three (a Dutchman, a Nigerian and an Indian) were all accidental victims of explosions or crossfire. Other victims include a Pakistani employee of the British Army who was shot by the IRA as a spy, an "asian" murdered by Protestant terrorists because they thought he was a member of the IRA, and a German whose killer is unknown. The only real act of "international terrorism" carried out by the IRA was the 1973 kidnap-murder of Herr Niedermayer, Managing Director of Grundig and acting West German consul in Belfast. While foreign-owned businesses have been bombed as part of the IRA's strategy of disrupting the economy, there is no sign that they have been singled out. ETA kidnapped the West German consul, in December 1970, and attempted to kidnap the French consul in May, 1971. A few foreign tourists were injured when ETA set off bombs in coastal resorts in the Summer of 1979.

Since leftist terrorism has resulted in far fewer deaths than nationalist terrorism, deaths from terrorism would be an inappropriate indicator. Instead, for Italy, the measure of terrorist activity is the sum of those killed and wounded in terrorist attacks plus other shooting incidents, kidnapping and robberies. For Uruguay, the measure is the sum of terrorist incidents of all types. The monthly fluctuations in terrorist violence in each country are shown in figures 2-8.

CHAPTER 3

POLICIES AGAINST TERRORISM

Anti-terrorist policies can be classified into two types; those directed at the terrorists themselves and those directed against their supporters in the general population. The first policy examined is aimed at the terrorists, the next three policies against their supporters. The target of the last two policies is the terrorists, but their impact falls harshly on the general population. The six policies are:

(1.) Ceasefires and Negotiations with the Terrorists

(2.) Improving Economic Conditions

(3.) Making Reforms

(4.) Collective Punishments

(5.) Emergency Powers, and other anti-terrorist legislation

(6.) The use of the security forces.

Ceasefires and Negotiations with the Terrorists

Attempting to negotiate a settlement with the terrorists directly is tempting to politicians in a democratic society for several reasons. First the cultural ethos of such societies emphasizes the desirability of resolving conflicts through the give and take of negotiations rather than through the use of force. Second, terrorist leaders are the only group in society who can, if they so choose, stop terrorism with a simple command. Third, negotiations are usually accompanied by a

truce, which makes them intrinsically desirable.[1]
Since they are usually linked, ceasefires and negotiations will be considered together in this
analysis. The first matter considered is the reduction in violence during the ceasefire itself.
Since ceasefires usually break down due to terrorist intransigeance, we next examine the level
at which violence resumes to see whether truces
benefit the terrorists.

Ceasefires, whether mutually agreed to or
declared unilaterally by the terrorists, are
fairly common. There were three in Cyprus, two
in Uruguay, and so far there have been four in
Northern Ireland and three in Spain. None has
occurred in Italy.[2]

Usually ceasefires result in a significant
decline in the level of violence. To measure the
effect of a ceasefire, a simple comparison is
made with the period of the same duration
immediately preceding the ceasefire.[3]

---

[1]Crawshaw notes that when EOKA suspended
operations in August 1956 and called for negotiations with Makarios, "it was difficult for
the Cyprus authorities to continue full-scale
operations...faced with a gesture...certain to be
seen as conciliatory by the world outside"
(1978:188-9). To the Conservative government,
which began talks with the Provisional IRA in
January 1975, "a ceasefire was an improvement
over bombs in the underground" (Bell, 1979:416).

[2]The number would be even higher if
ceasefires by the smaller groups such as the
Official IRA or ETA politico-militar were
included.

[3]For example, if the ceasefire lasted one
month we examined the violence in the month
preceding the ceasefire; if the ceasefire was for
two months we looked at the violence for the two
previous months.

Table 4 shows violence during the ceasefire as a percentage of violence during the pre-ceasefire period for all twelve ceasefires. In half the cases, there was no violence during the ceasefire, and in only one case did the amount of violence increase. An alternative way of expressing the impact of ceasefires is to estimate the number of people who would have been killed during the ceasefire, if the rate of violence had persisted at the pre-truce level. Such measurements suggest that the truces in Cyprus saved 215 lives, and those in Spain 18. The three "good" truces in Northern Ireland resulted in 14 lives being saved.

These measures still understate the ability of the terrorist to turn violence on or off. Often, truces are defined in a restricted way. During the second and third EOKA truces, the execution of Greek Cypriot traitors continued, and there were frequent clashes with the Turks. The February 1975 truce between the Provisional IRA and the British Army was limited to those two organizations, and the Provisionals continued to attack loyalists and members of other republican groups. If the impact of these truces is recalculated in terms of the reduction in security force fatalities alone, all three show a significant decline (see second column of Table 5). The Cyprus truces may have saved the lives of 85 members of the security forces and the Northern Irish truce 23. However, it is difficult to justify a "truce" which merely results in a redirection of terrorist attacks, as was the case in Northern Ireland during 1975.[1]

Before responding to a ceasefire offer, the authorities should consider not only the extent to which terrorist violence will continue against different targets, but also the ability of the terrorist leadership to control its followers and

---

[1]During the truce the IRA killed 24 members of the security forces and 106 civilians. In the comparable period preceding the truce, the numbers were 47 and 44.

TABLE 4   THE EFFECTIVENESS OF CEASEFIRES IN REDUCING TERRORIST VIOLENCE

	Violence during ceasefire as % of violence during period preceding ceasefire	
	All Violence	Violence Against Security Forces[1]
EOKA ceasefires		
8/16/56-8/27/56	0.0	
3/14/57-3/2/58	5.3	0.0
8/4/58-9/1/58	50.0	22.2
Tupamaro ceasefires		
9/6/71-1/6/72	17.8	
6/1/72-7/25/72	0.09	
Provisional IRA ceasefires		
6/26/72-=7/9/72	38.4	
12/22/74-1/16/75	0.0	
2/10/75-2/12/76	145.0	51.1
12/23/76-12/28/76	0.0	
ETA-m ceasefires		
10/31/75-11/25/75	0.0	
10/4/79-10/25/79	60.0	
2/21/80-3/9/80	0.0	
Average all ceasefires	26.4	

[1]Only calculated for ceasefires restricted to security forces.

the response of other terrorist groups. Some
evidence suggests that when one terrorist group
observes a ceasefire, other terrorist groups increase their activity and that the longer a truce
persists the more likely is a splintering off by
militants.[1] However, our examination shows that,
in the short run at least, ceasefires are usually
effective in reducing terrorist activity.

Discussion between governments and terrorists
rarely lead to conflict resolution.[2] Terrorist
demands are radical and non-negotiable. Nationalist groups want changes in national sovereign-
ty, revolutionary groups want a revolution.
Since the terrorists are unwilling to settle for
anything less, it is impossible for any government to reach a settlement with them, short of
complete capitulation to their demands.[3] Thus
almost inevitably the talks end in failure, and
the ceasefire breaks down. The question that
must next be discussed is what the consequences

---

[1]The Official IRA has observed a truce since
May 1972 but frustrated militants broke away in
December 1974 to form the Irish National Liberation Army, which promptly launched its own campaign against the British.

[2]In Cyprus a compromise settlement was
reached by negotiations between the United Kingdom, Greece, and Turkey. However, this settlement was possible only because of the division in
Cyprus between political and military leadership
roles. Makarios, the political leader, feared
partition if he did not accept the agreements and
abandon enosis. Grivas makes it clear that EOKA
"would never have accepted the terms" if they had
been at the London meetings. He only acquiesced
in what he viewed as a betrayal, because not to
do so would have led to "national division in
which...we would lose all." (Grivas, 1965:179-
203, 212-217)

[3]MacStiofain (1975:272) defines the IRA
position succinctly. "If the British refused our
proposals when negotiations began, the truce would
end and the campaign would be resumed."

of the ceasefire are after it is over. Does the
violence merely resume at the old level or does
one side gain from the truce?

Some writers argue that ceasefires are dangerous because they allow the terrorists to re-
build their military strength, as well as to en-
hance their public image. Crawshaw claims that
in Cyprus prior to the March 1957 truce "EOKA's
defeat seemed imminent" and that "the guerrillas
were on the verge of collapse." However, after
the year-long truce "the rebel movement which
faced the administration in 1958 was stronger and
even more fanatical...The long respite of the
ceasefire had enabled EOKA to build up its military strength" (Crawshaw, 1978:234, 236, 279).
There were also significant consequences in terms
of public opinion. "Cypriots who ... had begun
to cooperate with the British, were baffled and
afraid, and information which until then had been
readily forthcoming, ceased to reach the security
forces" (Crawshaw, 1978:236).

An almost identical argument is made by Wilkinson concerning the February 1975 truce in
Northern Ireland. He claims that "with the benefit of hindsight it is now possible to see that
the army had practically beaten the Provisional
IRA by December 1974. Hence the Provos' Christmas
truce and their so-called ceasefire proffered in
January 1975 were declared from a position of
desperate weakness. They had been decimated as a
military force and they urgently needed time to
lick their wounds, recruit and train new members,
await the release of their key men from internment and regroup" (Wilkinson, 1977:155).

As a result of the agreement between the British government and the Provisional IRA, the security forces were restricted in several ways;
their intelligence gathering activities were ham-
pered, internment was ended and the government

imposed constraints on their ability to open
fire. Furthermore, in order to monitor the
ceasefire, eight "incident centers" run by the
Provisional IRA were set up in Catholic areas.
These played a crucial local role, bypassing the
elected politicians who felt that "local control
had been turned over to the Provos" (Bell, 1979:
420).

The arguments made by Crawshaw and Wilkinson
seem applicable only to the longer truces. In
the eight truces which lasted less than a month,
the violence level was not noticeably affected by
the truce. If we compare the violence in the
month before the truce to the violence in the
month after the truce, there was a rise in four
cases and a decline in the other four. For all
cases together the average number of fatalities
in the month preceeding the truce was 12.9, and
in the month following the truce 11.5. In the
year-long truces, one in Cyprus and one in Northern Ireland, the terrorists did appear to benefit
from the truce. In both cases there was a sharp
decline in terrorist activity in the three to
four month period immediately preceding the
truce. EOKA killings fell from 34 in November
1956 to 8 in February 1957. In Northern Ireland,
comparing November 1974 with January 1975, explosions fell from 49 to 24, attacks on the security
forces from 123 to 37 and IRA killings from 15 to
4. This downward trend seems to have begun about
a year before the truce in the case of Northern
Ireland. Figure 1 shows the violence levels before and after the truces, for the year before
the truce and the year after the truce for Cyprus
and Northern Ireland. Statistics are given for
each three month period. In Northern Ireland IRA
killings and explosions resumed at a higher level
than before the truce, and in Cyprus the violence
shows a marked upward trend.

Thus our analysis suggests that negotiating a
truce with the terrorists is a short-sighted policy. Negotiations will not lead to resolution of
the conflict, and if the ceasefire is protracted
the terrorists rather than the government are the
gainers.

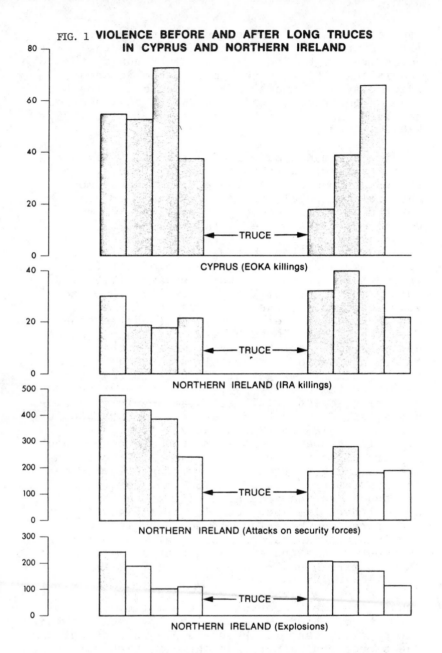

FIG. 1 **VIOLENCE BEFORE AND AFTER LONG TRUCES IN CYPRUS AND NORTHERN IRELAND**

CYPRUS (EOKA killings)

NORTHERN IRELAND (IRA killings)

NORTHERN IRELAND (Attacks on security forces)

NORTHERN IRELAND (Explosions)

NOTES: Violence measured for three-month periods for the year before and after the Northern Irish truce of February 1975 — February 1976 and the Cyprus truce of March 1957 — March 1958. The ending of the Cyprus campaign in December 1958 means that there are only three post-truce quarters.

42

Economic Conditions

There is a considerable body of literature to suggest that economic conditions are an important factor in social conflict. Conflict is more frequent and severe in poor societies than rich ones, a situation plausibly attributed to the struggle for scarce resources (Lipset, 1960; Gurr, 1970). Within a given society the well-to-do are more likely than the poor to be satisfied with and support the status quo. Adverse economic conditions have been linked to outbreaks of violence in several countries (Tilly, 1975; Rude, 1964).

In three of the five cases we examine, a plausible argument can be made that bad economic conditions are at the root of the trouble. Northern Ireland has a low standard of living and a high unemployment rate, and the IRA and their active supporters are from the most economically deprived section of the society. Boyle argues that working class Catholics are relatively disadvantaged in terms of employment, income and housing. This situation produced a "strong feeling of continuing deprivation and discrimination...and creates a fertile environment for continuing recruitment by the IRA" (1980:12-13). In Uruguay and Italy the growth of terrorism occurred during a period of economic decline, when both unemployment and the inflation rate rose steeply. Although neither the Tupamaros nor the Italian terrorists were drawn to any significant extent from the ranks of the poorest class, they attracted considerable support from the educated middle class whose career prospects were diminished by the stagnant economy.

However, the appeal of EOKA in Cyprus was manifestly free of any economic appeals. Indeed, economic conditions were such that one Enosist slogan was "better poor with Mother Greece than rich with Stepmother England" (Markides, 1977: 17). It is also difficult to argue that the Basques were economically deprived since the region was the richest in Spain,[1] and within the

---

[1] In 1975, Vizcaya had the highest per capita income of any province, while Guipuzcoa was ranked third.

Basque provinces, ethnic Basque are better off than non-Basques. A further point against the economic deprivation argument, in the case of ETA, is that the middle class was overrepresented in their ranks and there were very few unemployed ETA members.

In only one of the five cases, Northern Ireland, was there any significant attempt to ameliorate economic conditions. Boyle notes that in addition to a variety of anti-discrimination policies the UK government "made strenuous efforts to remedy the situation" by creating new jobs in the areas of highest unemployment. One well-known project was the DeLorean Motor Company which provided over 2000 jobs in Catholic areas of West Belfast, at a cost of £80 million in government loans and grants. The level of public spending in Northern Ireland has grown much more rapidly than in other parts of the United Kingdom (Boyle, 1980:9-12).[1]

While it is difficult to show that particular economic policies are responsible for the state of the economy, it is comparatively easy to measure the effect of economic conditions themselves on the level of violence. The latter type of analysis will suggest whether it is worthwhile trying to improve economic conditions in order to reduce terrorism. Three economic indicators, unemployment, cost of living and income were collected, if available on a monthly basis, for all five cases. Unemployment data exist for all five, cost of living data for all except Northern Ireland, and income data only for Uruguay and Spain.

---

[1] Excluding any military component, the payments by the United Kingdom to Northern Ireland, over and above the province's own tax revenues, rose from £52 million in 1966 to £313 million in 1975 (Utley, 1975:154). Public spending for non-military purposes totalled £2436 million in 1984, with about 40% coming from London.

First, we examine the correlation between violence levels and economic conditions for the same months. The Pearson correlation coefficients are shown below in column one of Table 5, with significant correlations starred.[1] Second, since it might be argued that economic conditions have a delayed rather than an immediate impact, we lagged the data for one through six months, and present the strongest lagged correlations in column two of Table 5.

The results, contrary to expectations, show that bad economic conditions are rarely linked to terrorism. Instead we usually find either that there is no significant link or that terrorism is higher during good economic conditions. If we consider the same-month correlations between terrorism and economic conditions, the relationship is not significant in five cases, and in seven cases terrorism is linked to good economic conditions (low unemployment in Northern Ireland and Uruguay, high income and salaries in Uruguay and Spain and low consumer price index in Uruguay). Only in Spain is the expected relationship found with bad economic conditions. The lagged correlations are very similar to the same-month correlations and in only two cases do non-significant correlations become significant. In Cyprus a rise in the consumer price index is linked to a rise in terrorism five months later. In Italy a rise in the index is associated with a decline in terrorism four months later.

It is striking that the only two countries where terrorism is associated with poor economic conditions (Spain and Cyprus) are the cases where it is most difficult to argue that the conflict

---

[1]A "significant" correlation is conventionally taken to be one that has a probability of happening by chance less than one time in twenty.

TABLE 5   ASSOCIATION BETWEEN ECONOMIC CONDITIONS AND TERRORIST VIOLENCE

	Same Month	Best Lag	Length of Best Lag
Northern Ireland (explosions)			
Unemployment	-.24*	-.27*	6 months
Northern Ireland (attacks on s.f.)			
Unemployment	-.28*	-.28*	1 month
Northern Ireland (IRA killings)			
Unemployment	-.03	-.12	5 months
Uruguay (all terrorist incidents)			
Unemployment	-.27*	-.24*	5 months
Real Income, Private Sector	.46*	.45*	4 months
Real Income, Public Sector	.47*	.42*	2 months
Consumer Price Index	-.43*	-.51*	6 months
Cyprus (EOKA killings)			
Unemployment	.06	-.03	4 months
Consumer Price Index	.14	.28*	5 months
Spain (ETA killings)			
Unemployment	.64*	.54*	1 month
Salaries	.33*	.58*	3 months
Consumer Price Index	.55*	.61*	1 month
Italy (killings, woundings and kidnappings)			
Unemployment	-.17	.10	4 months
Consumer Price Index	.06	-.28*	4 months

Note: Statistics shown are Pearsonian correlation coefficients. Starred if significant at the P .05 level. A negative sign indicates that as the value of the independent variable increases, terrorist violence declines.

was rooted in economic grievances. Any relationship in these countries is probably attributable
to the impact of protracted terrorism on the
economy.[1]

We conclude therefore that our analysis does
not support the view that an ongoing terrorist
campaign can be checked by improving general economic conditions. Two caveats should be entered
at this point. First, while economic reforms do
not reduce ongoing violence, they may prevent violence if carried out in time. Second, while
general economic amelioration has no effect, improving the economic situation of particular
groups (e.g. Belfast Catholics, unemployed university graduates) might be efficacious.

Making Reforms

It is a well established view that violence
is a result of popular grievances, and that one
way to reduce violence is to remove the grievance
by making reforms. By making reforms it is hoped
to win over the terrorists' supporters among the
general population, thus "drying up the water" in
which the terrorist fish swim. In Uruguay and
Italy there was no attempt at making the kind of
reforms, which could be effective in reducing
support for terrorism.[2] The British promised

---

[1]Political uncertainty and terrorism in the
Basque provinces of Guipuzcoa and Vizcaya led to
a massive flight of capital from the region.
"Factory after factory closed down after 1975, as
hundreds of industrialists...picked up and ran to
escape ETA's fund raising methods: abductions,
killings (and)...a steep "Revolutionary Tax" ex-
tracted on threat of death" (Sterling, 1981:181).

[2]About two thirds of Italians according to a
recent l'Espresso poll op cit believed that
"social reforms were necessary to weaken terrorism." Bell (1978:259) says that "Italy faces not
so much a terrorist problem as a need to restruc-
ture its society" and Silj (1979:xix-xx) believes
that urban terrorism will increase unless Italy
moves towards "social justice and...economic and
social growth." For a list of problems in Italian society see Bell (1978:237, 244) and Silj
(1979:200-204).

to finance a development plan for Cyprus that
would make it "the most prosperous island in the
Mediterranean" but the plan was never implement-
ed. Throughout the insurgency a number of constitutional changes were proposed by the British,
all of which excluded enosis and tried to balance
the conflicting interests and aspirations of the
United Kingdom, Greece, Turkey and the two Cypriot communities. The outcome is well summed up
by Crawshaw: "By 1958 almost every constitutional formula within the range of the human in-
tellect had been discussed time and again by the
parties concerned, amended and finally rejected
by at least one of them" (Crawshaw, 1978:275).

However, in both Northern Ireland and the
Basque provinces the authorities acknowledged
that changes had to be made in the status quo,
and embarked on a significant reform program.

In Northern Ireland the Cameron Commission,
set up by the British government to study the
situation in the aftermath of the riots of 1968,
concluded that "social and economic grievances or
abuses of political power were in a very real
sense an immediate and operative cause of the
demonstrations and consequent disorders" (Cameron
Commission, 1969:48). There is a general consensus as to the nature of the grievances. Politically a disproportionate number of Catholics were
denied a vote in local government elections, and
in a number of cases, local government ward boundaries were gerrymandered in favor of Protestants. Protestant councils discriminated against
Catholics in the allocation of housing and jobs,
Protestant firms discriminated against Catholics,
which together with a development policy that
largely ignored Catholic areas, resulted in high
rates of Catholic unemployment (Rose, 1971;
Cameron Commission, 1969).

The reforms fell into two groups,; first
there were the administrative changes and acts of
legislation by which the government manifestly
removed many of the Catholic disabilities. The
Electoral Law Act abolished plural voting and
introduced universal adult suffrage. The Local

48

Government Act set up a Ward Boundaries Commis
sion to insure that there would be no gerryman
dering. A Parliamentary Commissioner was
appointed to handle citizens grievances. The
Housing Executive, established to take over th
powers of local councils and develop a "points
system" to allocate public housing fairly, beg
meeting in May 1971. Catholic complaints that
police force was biased against them were met
disarming the police and abolishing the B Specials.[1] All these can be termed "civil rights
reforms" since they were designed to meet the
mands of the civil rights movement.

The second set of reforms attempted by con
stitutional adjustments to break the Protesta
monopoly of executive power. Two major acts e
body this policy: first the suspension of the
Northern Irish Parliament at Stormont on March
24, 1972 and its replacement by the direct rul
of United Kingdom civil servants, second the C
stitution Act of March 1973, which provided fo
return of a form of self government to Norther
Ireland. Certain legislative functions were t
be returned to a Northern Ireland Assembly and
executive functions were given to a Northern I
land Executive. A novel feature of this plan w
"power-sharing" between Protestants and Catholics. To end the dominant power of the all-Pr
testant Unionist party the act stipulated that
the Secretary of State for Northern Ireland wou
not sanction an executive consisting only of a
party supported by one community (Rose, 1976:29
By guaranteeing a significant role to Catholics
in the Northern Irish system, it was hoped to
gain their support and allegiance with a consequent reduction in Catholic violence. The

-----

[1]The B Specials were set up in 1920 as an
auxiliary police force. Exclusively Protestant,
they gained a reputation for anti-Catholic
bigotry and were accused of attacking civil
rights marchers in 1969.

power-sharing executive broke down in May 1974.[1]
The United Kingdom government later set up a Constitutional Convention for which elections were
held on May 1, 1975. The convention having failed to agree on a system of government for the
province, it was dissolved on March 5, 1976.

The Basques under the Franco regime had several grievances. They were forbidden to use
their language, or to manifest their identity by
celebrating their national day (Aberri Eguna) or
flying their national flag (the Ikurrina). They
were denied political autonomy, and, like other
Spaniards, lacked all democratic rights. Indeed
the Basques suffered more under Franco than any
other group in Spain, and constituted an altogether disproportionate share of those in prison
for political offenses.

Even as Franco lay dying, the situation began to
change. In November 1975 a decree was issued
tolerating regional languages, in December 1978
the constitution declared regional languages
co-official with Spanish, and in January 1978 the
teaching of the Basque language in the schools
was extended. The Ikurrina was tolerated by order of the Minister of the Interior in September
1976, whereupon just under half of the municipal-
ities in the Basque region began to fly it along-
side the Spanish flag. The first legal celebra-
tion of Aberri Eguna was in 1978. By a series of
amnesties in November 1975, July 1976, March
1977, and May 1977 all the Basque political prisoners were given their freedom.

Beginning in May 1976, when political asso-
ciations were allowed, Spain moved steadily
towards democracy; the first free elections were
held in June 1977 and the new constitution came
into effect on December 28, 1978. Discussions on
Basque autonomy began in September 1977, the

---

[1]Loyalists objected to the setting up of a
"Council of Ireland," and to being forced to
share power with "republicans." By industrial ac-
ion they paralyzed the province and brought a-
out the downfall of the power-sharing executive.
'or a full account see Fisk (1975).

autonomy statute was formulated in July 1979, approved by a referendum in the Basque provinces in October 1975, and finally, in March 1980, elections were held for a Basque parliament.

If it is true that making reforms reduces violence, then we should find, in the period after the reforms have been made, a lower rate of violence than in the period prior to the reforms. This proposition is easier to formulate than to apply. There is the problem of deciding what constitutes "making a reform" when the reform process goes through several stages. The level of alienation among Northern Irish Catholics and Spanish Basques, makes it highly unlikely that promises of reform, discussions or study commissions will have much effect, so we will consider only legislation or administrative changes. The violence levels for Northern Ireland and Spain are shown relative to the chronology of reforms in Tables 6 and 7.

The changes in the rate of violence are easier to understand if the political context of the reforms is taken into account. We do this by dividing the reform process into a series of phases.

In the first phase an unpopular regime with a history of repression was visibly in crisis. In Spain the crisis was brought about by the illness and death of Franco, in Northern Ireland by the civil rights campaign, the communal rioting and the arrival of the British Army. In both countries the government tried to reduce opposition by making concessions. The concessions did not reduce violence in either country; in Spain the violence held steady, in Northern Ireland it increased. The concessions were ineffective because they were viewed as tokens, and as long overdue. Even more important, they were seen as a sign of weakness. People were emboldened to demand more, once the regime failed to repress dissent forcefully, as in the past.

The first phase ended for Northern Ireland with the suspension of Stormont (in March 1975) and for Spain with the first post-Franco elections (June 1977). At this point it was

51

TABLE 6 REFORM CHRONOLOGY AND VIOLENCE IN NORTHERN IRELAND

Reform	IRA Killings (Monthly Average)
January 1970-January 1971 Electoral Law Act (one man-vote, Ward Boundaries Commission)	0.5
February 1971 Housing Executive set up	4.5
June 1971 Anti- Discrimination clause in Government Contracts	8.2
March 1972 Suspension of Stormont/Direct Rule	13.3
March 1973 Constitution Act	17.1
May 1973 First Local Council Elections under new system	10.0
May 1974 Fall of Power Sharing Executive	8.1
May 1975 Constitutional Convention Elections	7.3
March 1976 Dissolution of Constitutional Convention	12.6
January 1977 Fair Employment Agency established	10.2
December 1980	15.5

Note: The figures given are the monthly averages for the period ending at the date specified, and beginning at the previous date.

52

TABLE 7 REFORM CHRONOLOGY AND VIOLENCE IN BASQUES PROVINCES

Reform	ETA Killings (Monthly Average)
January 1975-November 1975 Regional Languages Tolerated	1.4
June 1976 Political Parties allowed	2.0
September 1976 Ikurrina tolerated	0.3
June 1977 First elected Spanish Parliament	1.0
December 1977 Pre-autonomy status granted to Basques Provinces	0.8
February 1978 Basque General Council set up	0.5
December 1978 Final approval of Democratic Constitution, Regional languages cofficial with Spanish	6.4
March 1979 Elections to Spanish Parliaments, Provincial Assemblies and Municipal Elections	10.5
October 1979 Approval of Basque Autonomy Statute	5.8
March 1980 Elections to Basque Parliament	5.6
December 1981	4.8

Note: The figures given are the monthly averages for the period ending at the date specified, and beginning at the previous date.

clear that the old regime was finished, and a new one in the process of creation. In this second phase when new institutions were being shaped, violence reached a peak in both societies. Such violence by the terrorists was a rational strategy, a means of attracting attention and ensuring that their views were not ignored.

The conclusion of this phase came in March 1973 in Northern Ireland with the Constitution Act, and in October 1979 in Spain with the approval of the Basque Autonomy Statute. In both countries, as of these dates, the moderates were granted almost every one of their demands. Northern Irish Catholics had achieved one man-one vote, a reformed system of housing allocation, the abolition of gerrymandering, and a guaranteed role in the government. The Basques had achieved cultural-linguistic freedom, democratic rights and regional autonomy. From this point on, one would expect therefore a decline in violence, and such was the case in Spain. In Northern Ireland, the post-reform period lasted for just over a year until the power-sharing executive collapsed. During the post-reform period violence declined and, surprisingly, continued to decline even after the end of power-sharing. The second attempt to create a new political system through a Constitutional Convention led to another increase in terrorism. Thereafter violence declined somewhat erratically.

Reforms then do affect the level of violence but they do so in a complex fashion. Policy makers should anticipate that concessions made from a position of weakness will increase violence, and that during the creation of new institutions terrorist groups will be very active. Not until several years after the start of a reform program will the violence start to decline. Finally one should note that even after significant changes have been made in Northern Ireland and the Basque provinces, terrorism still remains a major problem in both areas.[1]

---

[1]Clark (1984:274) suggests that ETA violence may persist because of the "slowness of or the incompleteness of gains made by moderate Basque nationalists."

Collective Punishments

Collective punishments, in which the civilian population of a given area is held responsible for acts of violence taking place within that area, have been used throughout history. However, collective punishment was employed in only one of the five cases considered in this analysis.

In Cyprus under the Emergency Powers (Collective Punishment) Regulations, 1955, district commissioners, with the approval of the governor, could impose four kinds of sanctions. They could:

1. order that a fine be levied on the assessable inhabitants of the area;

2. order that all or any of the shops in the area be closed during such times and under such conditions as specified;

3. order the seizure of any moveable or immoveable property of any inhabitant of the area;

4. order that all or any dwelling houses in the area be closed and kept closed and unavailable for human habitation for such period or periods as specified.

These powers were used quite sparingly. Fines were levied on twelve occasions, shops were closed four times, and buildings requisitioned twice. The clause allowing the seizure of property was invoked on only one occasion. Since some locations were punished more than once and in more than one way, only fourteen areas (five towns and nine villages) experienced collective punishments A complete listing is given in Table 8.

Before testing for the deterrent effect of collective punishments, one must make certain assumptions about the distribution of violence between areas and the likely impact of collective punishment. One assumption might be that violence would be randomly distributed throughout the Greek Cypriot areas. This, however, is implausible since we know that EOKA was strong in certain areas, weak in others.

TABLE 8   COLLECTIVE PUNISHMENTS IN CYPRUS

Area	Date	Sanction
Lefkoniko	4 December 1955	£ 2000
Ypsonas	4 December 1955	£ 200
Paralimni	4 December 1955	£ 1500
Nicosia	16 March 1956	Eviction
Lapithos	19 March 1956	£ 7000
Yialoussa	19 March 11956	£ 2000
Phrenaros	28 March 1956	£ 1500
Kalopsida	10 April 1956	£ 1000
Nicosia	18 April 1956	Closing/Property
Limassol	20 April 1956	Closing
Paphos	13 May 1956	£ 5500
Nicosia	25 May 1956	Eviction
Pano	28 May 1956	£ 3000
Zodhia	28 May 1956	£ 3000
Famagusta	1 June 1956	£ 40,000
Limassol	22 June 1956	£ 35,000
Nicosia	28 September 1956	Closing
Kyrenia	28 September 1956	Closing

Notes: Size of fine given in Cyprus pounds, then equivalent to just
under $3.00. "Closing refers to shop closing, "Eviction" to the
eviction of people from their homes and "Property" to property
seizure.

According to Grivas, there were seventy-five village bands, i.e., only about one in six Greek villages had an EOKA unit. In relation to the size of the Greek population in the six major towns, EOKA's strength was greatest in Famagusta, lowest in Larnaca.[1] There was a definite tendency for certain places to have a history of violence and indeed this was the justification for punishing them.[2]

Collective punishments might reduce the violence in the area which was punished, in the areas surrounding and even in Cyprus as a whole. However, it seems most plausible to assume that the greatest effect will be found in the area punished, and we shall test first for this local effect. The test is as follows: for each urban place where a collective punishment was imposed we calculate the amount of violence in that area as a percentage of total violence throughout the island, before and after the punishment. If the proportion of violence occurring in that area decreases, it suggests that collective punishments do deter. On the other hand, if the proportion remains constant it suggests that collective punishments are ineffectual or even, if the proportion increases, that collective punishments are counter-productive. In Table 9, the statistics are given for each of the five towns and for the nine villages in aggregate: the nine villages have been considered together because the amount of violence in any one is such a small fraction of total violence in the whole island. The table

-----

[1]A comparison of EOKA strength (Grivas, 1965:66-67) with the 1960 Census shows that for every 10,000 Greeks there were 31 guerrillas in Famagusta and only 4 in Larnaca.

[2]When the village of Lefkoniko was fined, the Governor paid a personal visit and warned the inhabitants that they had "a very bad record."

TABLE 9   THE EFFECTIVENESS OF COLLECTIVE PUNISHMENTS IN CYPRUS

Place	Violence in Area as % of Violence in all Cyprus		
	Before Collective Punishment	After Collective Punishment	Change
First Punishment			
Nicosia	40.8	17.9	-22.0
Famagusta	19.2	13.2	-6.0
Limassol	13.7	8.0	-5.7
Paphos	7.6	6.6	-1.0
Kyrenia	2.1	1.3	-0.8
Villages[1]	4.4	1.4	-3.0
Subsequent Punishments			
Nicosia	17.9	35.7	+17.8
Limassol	8.0	11.5	+ 3.5
Nicosia	35.7	32.4	- 3.3
Nicosia	32.4	28.2	- 4.2

Average net change = -2.16

[1]All violence in Lefkoniko, Ypsonas, Paralimni, Lapithos, Yhialoussa, Phrenaros, Kalopsida, Pano and Zodhia aggregated before and after last collective punishment 28 May, 1956.

distinguishes between the impact of the first collective punishment and any subsequent ones.[1]

The figures support the view that collective punishments do reduce violence, in the areas which are punished,the first time they are imposed. In Nicosia and Limassol the impact is most apparent while in Paphos and Kyrenia, there is only a very slight reduction. It should be noted, however, that when collective punishments are repeated they have less impact, and in some cases a rise in violence ensues. Considering all cases together the average reduction is -2.6%.

It could be argued that these reductions are spurious because when an area is punished, the terrorists become more active in adjacent areas. Thus all that a collective punishment does is to move the violence from one place to another, without reducing the overall level. To test for this the statistics were recalculated for the area within a ten mile radius of each town.[2] This reanalysis does suggests that some of the decline, in the areas where collective punishments were imposed, is offset by an increase in violence in the surrounding areas. Even so the effect of collective punishments is still to reduce violence overall; the average reduction being -1.7%.

---

[1]When more than one collective punishment was imposed on a town, the "before" and "after" periods are defined as follows, when A is the beginning of the period, B the first collective punishment, C the second collective punishment and D the end of the period. The "before" periods for the first punishment runs from A to B, the "after" period from B to C. The "before" period for the second punishment runs from B to C and the "after" period from C to D.

[2]A map put out by the Cyprus National Struggle Museum shows the location of violent incidents during the EOKA campaign.

These findings are unexpected since writers
on both sides argue that collective punishments
alienated the population and increased sympathy
for the guerrillas. Grivas claims that "village
after village was made to pay sums ranging from a
few £100 to as much as £7,000...The British
kept this practice up for six months until...they
realized that the only result of their actions
was to turn the people still further against
them" (Grivas, 1965:68). Paget (1967: 146) concludes that "the policy of collective punishment
did not succeed in turning the people away from
EOKA, and was widely criticized as doing more
harm than good...in that it aroused bitterness
among the uncommitted element of the populace and
alienated potential good will." Our analysis
does not support these arguments; collective punishments were certainly not counterproductive.
Even if the policy increased popular resentment
against the British they apparently made the
Greek Cypriots more reluctant to help EOKA.[1]

---

[1]It may be that such effects are not
likely to occur in other societies. Loizos'
study (1975) of Greek Cypriot villagers shows
them to be highly calculating and rational and
centuries of Ottoman rule had accustomed them to
the concept of communal responsibility.

Emergency Powers and Anti-Terrorist Legislation

Terrorism is much more likely to occur in liberal-democratic states than under authoritarian or totalitarian regimes (Laqueur, 1977: 131-148). Unfortunately democracies face the dilemma that the powers which sustain tyranny are the same emergency powers which they need to defeat terrorism. The general nature of these powers is suggested by their names, "Prompt Security Measures" in Uruguay, "Special Powers" in Northern Ireland and "State of Exception" in Spain. Emergency powers can be classified into a variety of categories and serve several functions. Typically in an emergency situation, the government controls the possession of firearms, requires civilians to carry identity cards, grants the security forces additional powers to arrest, search and curfew the population, restricts due process for those suspected of terrorist offenses and limits the exercise of political rights. We discuss the rationale for each of these powers in turn, and describe the variation between the five cases.

1. Controls on firearms are normal practice in most societies and while terrorists can obtain weapons through other channels, it is common sense to make their legal acquisition as difficult as possible. In Cyprus and Uruguay strict controls were imposed and many privately held weapons confiscated.[1]

2. Requiring the population to carry identity cards is also standard in several countries. The value of such a system to the security forces is clear. "With a system of identity cards showing photograph, finger-prints and signature, the Security Forces would be able to look at the suspect's card and know that the person questioned was, at least in all probability, who he claimed to be" (Evelegh, 1978:126). In Italy and Spain identity cards were required even before the current outbreak of terrorism, and in Cyprus and Uruguay were

---

[1] By an order issued January 24, 1956 all private guns in Cyprus were confiscated. The previous night EOKA gunmen had gone door to door in many villages, and obtained more than 200 guns.

introduced during the emergency. Surprisingly no civil registration system is in effect in Northern Ireland.[1]

  3. The security forces are allowed to arrest and question people without charge, to search houses and to impose curfews. Evelegh's justification of these arrest powers is that "there was no other way...to find out who the people living in the terrorist-affected areas were, what they looked like or where they lived." Also those arrested could give information without it being known that they had cooperated with the security forces (Evelegh, 1978:120).

  4. Special courts and procedures are set up to try those accused of terrorist offences. Even more serious is detention without trial whereby people suspected of an offence can be imprisoned indefinitely. These denials of due process are usually defended on the grounds that witnesses and juries are being intimidated.[3] In Cyprus, according to the Annual Police Report (1956) intimidation was so great that Cypriots were "completely terrified to be seen even talking to a policeman." In Northern Ireland the Gardiner Committee was given "details of 482 instances of civilian witnesses...being too frightened to make any statement or go to court" (Evelegh, 1978:123). One trial of

---

[1]Maguire (1973:95) notes, however, that "British soldiers at road-blocks and at chance searches always asked for your papers. It was far simpler to present a driving license than to protest that you weren't obliged to carry papers."

[2]In Italy under the Cossiga Law of 1979, suspects may be held without trial for up to eleven years if the magistrate believes there are reasonable grounds for preventive detention.

[3]Another argument, put forward by the Diplock Committee in Northern Ireland, was that "unduly restrictive rules of evidence" should not prevent terrorists being convicted. The Diplock courts allow confessions, and signed evidence to be used, and place the burden of proof on the defendant if weapons were found.

Red Brigade terrorists was postponed twice because lawyers and jurors were afraid to serve on the case.[1]

5.   Anti-terrorist laws often impose draconian penalties upon those convicted of terrorist offences is the hope that this will serve as a deterrent.   In Cyprus capital punishment was introduced for the legal possession of firearms and whipping for offenders under 18; collective punishments could be levied on towns and villages. Italy, in December 1979, made life imprisonment mandatory for those convicted of killing a policeman; Spain, in August 1975, imposed the death penalty for acts causing the death of a member of the security forces, a government official or a kidnap victim.

6.   Political rights, such as free speech and the right of assembly, are often curtailed by the authorities, organizations banned and censorship imposed.   In Uruguay six leftist parties were banned, and 41 newspapers closed (11 permanently). The press was forbidden to use the word "Tupamaro" and prohibited from publishing any news of guerrilla activity, except that supplied by the government.   In Cyprus the government banned the Communist Party (AKEL), and two Church-related youth groups, OHEN and PEON.   All assemblies and demonstrations were also forbidden.   The Times of Cyprus was convicted land fined under a regulation prohibiting the publication of "any report or statement likely to cause alarm or despondency, or to be prejudicial to public safety or the maintenance of public order."   However, in Northern Ireland, Italy and post-Franco Spain only the most minor and

---

[1]In June 1976 the Red Brigade murdered Attorney General Coco and then threatened the jury with death, causing the first postponement of Curcio's trial.   On April 28, 1977 the president of the Turin Bar Association was killed and 36 potential jurors asked to be excused for "medical" reasons which led to the second postponement.

selective restrictions have been imposed.[1]
Indeed the Provisional Sinn Fein, and Herri
Batasuna, which are generally regarded as
political fronts for the IRA and ETA are allowed to
contest elections.

Table 10 presents a summary of the emergency
powers employed in each country. With the possible
exception of Italy, there is a basic similarity
although there are minor differences in the powers,
such as how long persons could be held without
charge. More importantly the table does not show
the length of time that the emergency powers were
in effect.

In figures 2-8 an attempt has been made to
suggest the severity of the powers at different
periods. The severity of the emergency powers is
represented by the height of the shaded areas; the
higher the shaded area the more extensive the powers. In constructing the index, six factors were
considered: detention without trial, harsh penalties for terrorist offences or sweeping definitions
of what constitutes terrorism, special courts,
arrest without charge, searches without a warrant,
and censorship. Powers that were legally granted
but never exercised were ignored. Detention without trial was scored five, everything else two. If
an emergency power was exercised in a mild form and
then a severe form, it was scored accordingly. The
indices constructed by these procedures are somewhat arbitrary, especially for making cross-national
comparisons.[2] For comparisons within a given
country over time they are a reasonably valid
measure of a government's repressive potential.

----

[1]Though it should be noted that several
Italian editors, journalists and lawyers were
arrested in early 1981 as "propagandists" or "sub-
versives," with no charge made that they had mater-
ially assisted the terrorists (See New York Times
1/2/81, 1/4/81, 2/14/81).

[2]Several academics specializing in such
matters were asked to rank the emergency powers in
importance, but no consensus could be obtained,
except that detention without trial was judged the
most severe deprivation of civil liberties.

TABLE 10 EMERGENCY POWERS AND ANTI-TERRORIST LEGISLATION BY COUNTRY

	Cyprus	Uruguay	N. Ireland	Spain	Italy
Compulsory civilian IDS.	+	+		+	+
Weapons control	+	+	+	+	+
Questioning without charge	+	+	+	+	+
House searches without warrant	+	+	+	+	+
Curfews	+	+	+		
Special courts	+	+	+	+	
Detention without trial	+	+	+	+	+
Increased penalties	+	+	+	+	+
Right of assembly restricted	+	+	+	+	
Organizations banned	+	+	+	+	
Censorship	+	+		+	
Collective punishment	+				

+ specified power in effect at some time during the period. For details see text.

By showing the emergency powers in effect for different periods, and superimposing on this diagram the terrorist activity indicator, we are able to examine the figures to see if there is any relationship between the two.

The most obvious connection is that emergency powers are usually enacted or made more severe as a response to an increase in violence. In Cyprus, the State of Emergency proclaimed November 1955 was described by the Governor as a response to the increase in terrorism (Crawshaw, 1978: 147). The State of Exception in the Basque provinces in April 1975 followed a series of attacks on the Guardia Civil. The Moro kidnapping of 1978 resulted in the enactment of severe anti-terrorist measures in Italy. Similarly when violence declines, emergency powers are often relaxed or done away with altogether. These facts suggest that emergency powers are, at least in part, symbolic. They are a way for the authorities to signal their recognition of the severity of the situation and their determination to do something about it. By relaxing or ending a state of emergency, the authorities signal their confidence that they have regained control of the situation.

The more significant question, of course, is whether the introduction of a state of emergency, or anti-terrorist legislation, causes a decline in the level of violence. None of the five cases displays any recognizable pattern whereby violence declines following the introduction of emergency powers. Sometimes violence declines,[1] sometimes

---

[1]Imposition of the death sentence in Cyprus in November 1956 supposedly reduced EOKA terrorism (Crawshaw, 1978:204).

it increases,[1] but most times the legislation has
no discernible impact. Nevertheless we should not
necessarily dismiss all emergency powers as ineffective. First one could argue that some emergency powers have an effect but not others; for example, capital punishment might work but not detention without trial.[2] This argument is difficult to
test, since most anti-terrorist legislation grants
the government a package of powers, and the individual effects of a particular policy cannot be iso-
lated. Second it could be objected that emergency
powers do work eventually, but that a long period
of time is required before they have an impact. The
problem here is deciding how long a lag-time is required. Certainly in some cases, such as Northern
Ireland, emergency conditions have been in effect
for lengthy periods without any noticeable impact
on the level of violence. A third argument seem
the most persuasive. Some reductions in the civil
liberties of the population are probably necessary
in order for the security forces to operate effectively against terrorism, but the crucial issue is
how these powers are used. The existence of a law
allowing detention without trial is not as important as how many people, and what kinds of people,
are imprisoned. In the next section, therefore, we
consider how the army, police and courts operate
against terrorism, within the context of the legal
powers granted to them.

---

[1]A much cited example is the dramatic
upsurge in violence following the introduction of
internment in Northern Ireland. Since it was used
only against Catholics and against many who were
not connected with the terrorists, it increased
support for the IRA. Clark (1984:273) points out
that ETA attacks increased after July 1978 when a
tough new anti-terrorist law was imposed. He
concludes that the new policy "did little if
anything to restrain or limit ETA violence."

[2]The most effective powers may not always
involve the most severe deprivations of civil
liberties. Evelegh comments that "for me,
detention without trial was an unnecessarily
massive erosion of liberty in Northern Ireland, and
as a security operator in the Upper Falls, I would
have happily traded it for compulsory identity
cards" (1978:61).

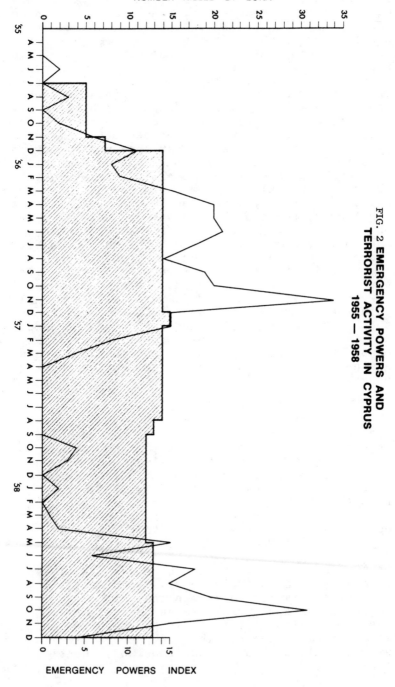

FIG. 2 EMERGENCY POWERS AND
TERRORIST ACTIVITY IN CYPRUS
1955 — 1958

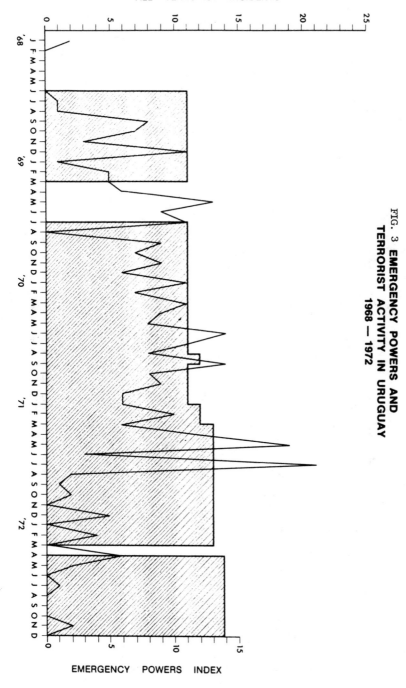

ALL TERRORIST INCIDENTS

FIG. 3 EMERGENCY POWERS AND
TERRORIST ACTIVITY IN URUGUAY
1968 — 1972

EMERGENCY POWERS INDEX

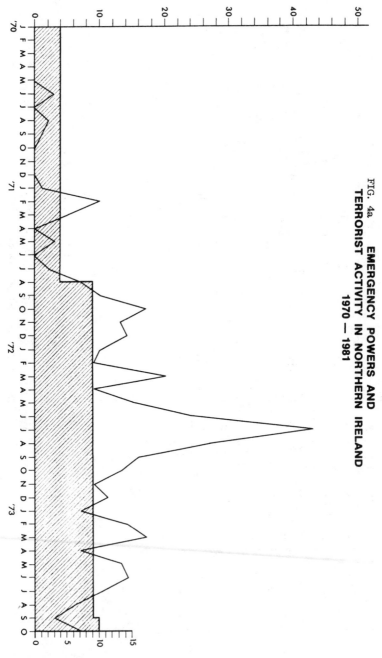

FIG. 4a   EMERGENCY POWERS AND
TERRORIST ACTIVITY IN NORTHERN IRELAND
1970 — 1981

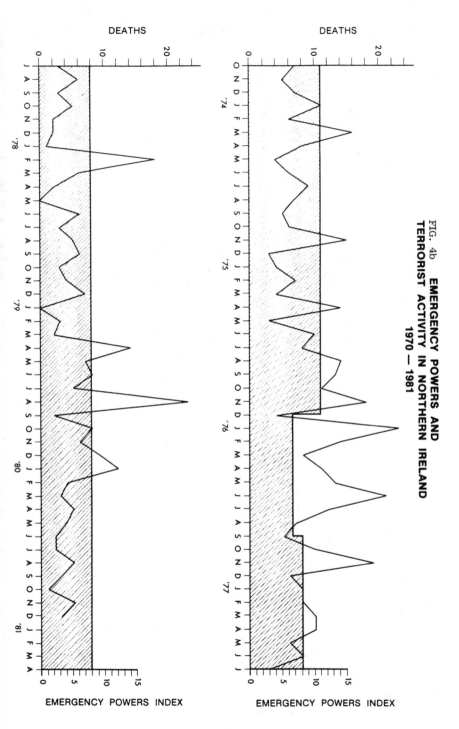

FIG. 4b **EMERGENCY POWERS AND TERRORIST ACTIVITY IN NORTHERN IRELAND 1970 — 1981**

71

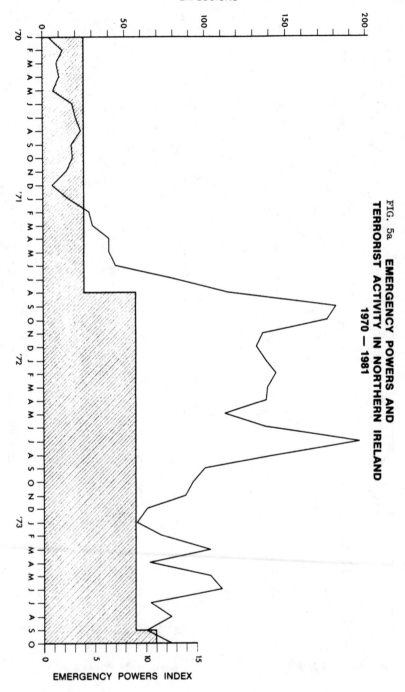

FIG. 5a   EMERGENCY POWERS AND
TERRORIST ACTIVITY IN NORTHERN IRELAND
1970 — 1981

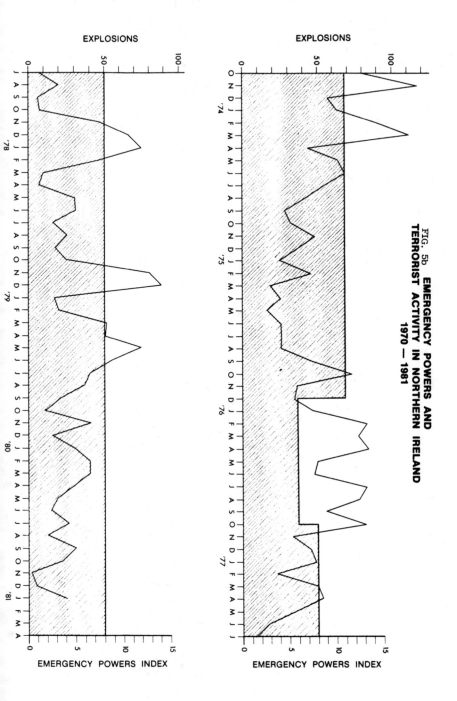

FIG. 5b EMERGENCY POWERS AND
TERRORIST ACTIVITY IN NORTHERN IRELAND
1970 — 1981

73

NUMBER OF INCIDENTS IN WHICH SECURITY FORCES WERE FIRED UPON

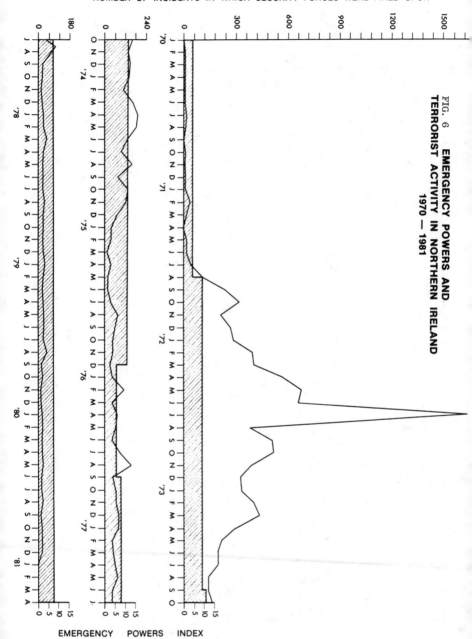

FIG. 6 EMERGENCY POWERS AND
TERRORIST ACTIVITY IN NORTHERN IRELAND
1970 — 1981

EMERGENCY POWERS INDEX

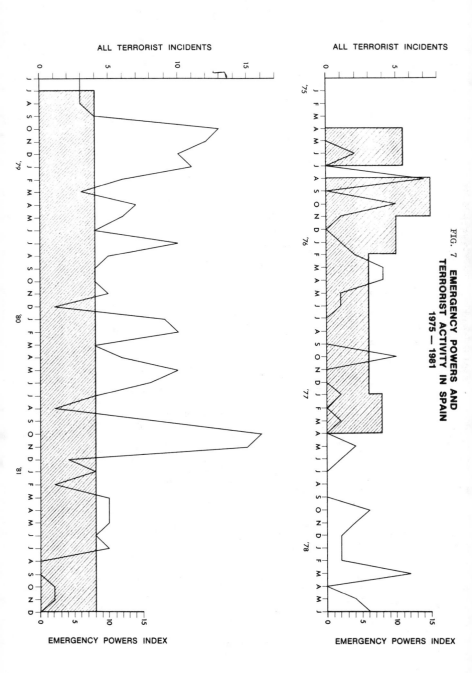

FIG. 7 EMERGENCY POWERS AND
TERRORIST ACTIVITY IN SPAIN
1975 — 1981

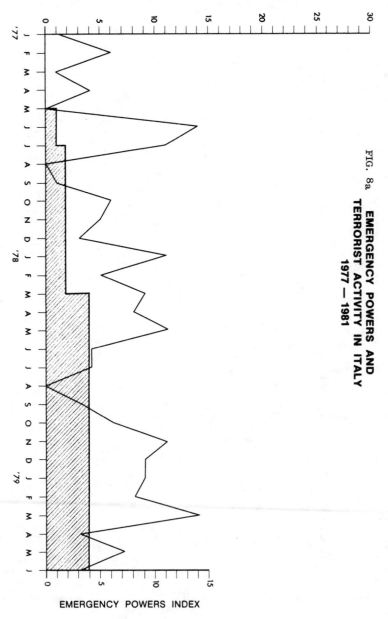

FIG. 8a

**EMERGENCY POWERS AND
TERRORIST ACTIVITY IN ITALY
1977 — 1981**

ALL TERRORIST INCIDENTS

EMERGENCY POWERS INDEX

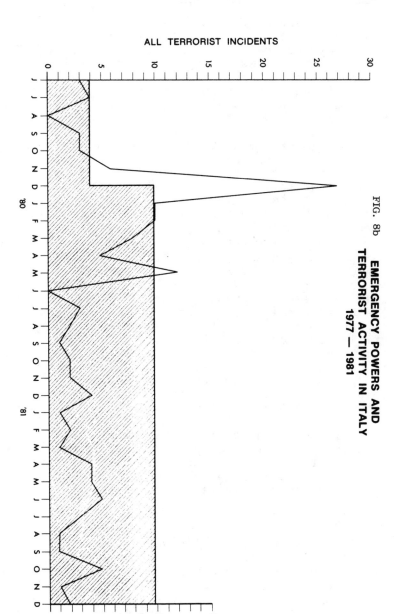

ALL TERRORIST INCIDENTS

FIG. 8b

EMERGENCY POWERS AND
TERRORIST ACTIVITY IN ITALY
1977 — 1981

EMERGENCY POWERS INDEX

77

The Use of the Security Forces

Even the most liberal state must rely, to some extent, upon the use of repressive force against terrorism. The significant role played by the security forces in any anti-terrorist struggle is indicated by the efforts made to increase their capabilities. Such efforts take various forms: numbers are increased, training is improved, structures are reorganized.

It is difficult to give a single statistic on the size of the anti-terrorist forces at any given time since a number of different groups may be involved in the counter insurgency effort to varying degrees. Sometimes the army is the main force in the war on terrorism, as in Cyprus and Northern Ireland.[1] In Italy the main role is played by the national police, the Carabinieri, and in Spain by a special paramilitary unit, the Guardia Civil. In Uruguay the police initially took the major role but later were supplanted by the army. Some units of the security forces, for example traffic police, are not involved in counterterrorist activity. Despite these problems it still seems worthwhile to present, in Table 11, some measure of the strength of the security forces in each of the five cases. The figures pertain to the period of maximum strength, and, in the final column, the ratio of security force personnel to the total population is calculated.

In colonies, or countries where violence is limited to certain regions, dramatic increases in security force strength are possible. In Cyprus the peace-time garrison was under 6,000 but this figure was doubled in less than six months when the

----

[1] In Northern Ireland under the policy of "Ulsterization," the local police and the Ulster Defence Regiment were given increased responsibilities for security. This is reflected in the casualty figures, which show that, during 1971-74, British soldiers constituted 69% of security force fatalities, but only 41% during 1975-82.

TABLE 11 SECURITY FORCE STRENGTH

	Military	Police	Auxiliaries	/1000 Population
Uruguay	16,000	17,000 (National) 5,000 (Local)		12
Cyprus	30,000	2,400	1,900 (Special constables)	60
Northern Ireland	21,000	4,200	2,500 (Police Reserve) 9,000 (Ulster Defence Regt)	24
Spain	210,000	62,000 (Guardia Civil) 32,000 (Policia Armada)		10
Basque Provinces[1]				36
Italy	307,000	80,000 (Carabinieri) 80,000 (Pubblica Sicurezza) 40,000 (Customs Police) 250,000 (Local)		14

Note:

1. Assumes one quarter of Spanish security forces deployed in Basque Provinces.

emergency was declared. In Northern Ireland the normal strength of the British army in the province, some 3,000, increased overnight to 5,800 when troops were deployed to halt communal rioting. In Spain when the Basques "seem restless, large numbers of extra police of all kinds are moved into the area."[1] However, the total strength of the Spanish security forces declined slightly throughout the period.[2] In Italy the combined strength of the Carabinieri and the Pubblica Sicurezza has remained constant at about 160,000. The Uruguayan armed forces increased from 12,000 in 1968 to 16,000 in 1970.

The counter-terrorist capabilities of the security forces can be improved by special training, by special equipment and by administrative reorganization. In Cyprus, the police force was totally unprepared to respond to a terrorist campaign, and indeed was heavily penetrated by EOKA. The British response was to appoint a new commissioner of police, to send in large numbers of British police officers to take over many key positions in the force, and to reorganize police procedures along British lines. A small number of Cypriot police attended training courses in the United Kingdom. The military, police and civil administration were coordinated by establishing a central joint staff and operations center. In each of the six districts, security committees, composed of the district commissioner, the senior police officer and the military commander were set up.

---

[1]According to an estimate given in Medhurst (1972:17) there were as many as 15,000 Guardia Civil in the area in 1970, that is one quarter of the force for 7% of Spain's population. Clark suggests that currently just under one fifth of the Guardia Civil are stationed in the region.

[2]The Guardia Civil numbered 62,000 in 1974 and 60,000 in 1980 while the Policia Armada declined from 32,000 to 25,000 during the same period.

In Uruguay during 1962-70 the national police received a large amount of money and training from abroad, mainly from the United States through the Agency for International Development.

> "Uruguay's law enforcement agencies were granted, over the 1961-71 period, more financial aid from the United States than any other of the 18 Latin American countries for which data are available...By 1971, 113 policemen had received training in the United States and over 700 had been trained in Uruguay" (Porzecanski, 1973:53).

There was increasing coordination between Uruguay's military and police as the terrorist threat worsened. In July 1969 the police were placed under military discipline, and in September 1971 the armed forces were officially put in charge of the entire anti-Tupamaro campaign. At the same date the prison system was put under the control of the military.

In Northern Ireland the anti-terrorist capabilities of the British army have been improved by the introduction of such technology as night vision, explosive-handling devices and computers. However, there is very little coordination between the security forces and the civil authorities (Evelegh, 1978:49-51, 112-113). The Royal Ulster Constabulary (RUC) were disarmed in October 1969 which presumably reduced their effectiveness. (They were rearmed in late 1970.)

During the transition to democracy after Franco's death, it is likely that the capabilities of the Spanish security forces were reduced by various reorganizations of the police system. High ranking officers identified with the Franco regime were replaced, the political police were abolished (October, 1976), and the Guardia Civil lost responsibility for public order in many towns

(June, 1977). However, in March 1978, a specially trained and equipped anti-terrorist police force was created, while later in the year an anti-ETA strike force was set up in Bilbao. This unit was able to infiltrate ETA and inflict severe damage on the organization (Clark, 1979:369-70).

In Italy during the early 1970's, police and intelligence agencies came under considerable criticism from Communist and Socialist politicians. The public image of the security forces was damaged by the Miceli scandal in which the director of SID was accused of being involved in two right-wing coup attempts. Consequently, in May 1976, the police were deliberately restricted and the department of public security was reorganized so that there was less coordination between the various intelligence agencies. However, matters improved in October 1977, when an Interministerial Committee on Intelligence and Security (CIIS) was established.[1] Parliament authorized increased expenditures ($117,000,000) for modern police equipment, and police salaries were increased substantially.

If Italy is excluded, there are marked similarities between the counterinsurgency policies pursued by the security forces in the different countries. The policies will be discussed under two headings, routine preventive measures and mass searches.

The most common tactics are for the security forces to guard, to patrol, and to stop and search individuals and vehicles at random. The goal of such tactics is to dominate terrorist-infiltrated areas, and to inhibit the movement and activities of the terrorists. Preventive tactics of this sort probably take up the major part of the time spent by the security forces in counter insurgency activities in all countries. They have two disadvantages; a great amount of effort must be expended

---

[1]A further coordination was effected in 1978. A central office, UCIGOS, was set up to oversee both non-military and military counter-intelligence, now renamed SISDE and SISMI respectively.

with only a small likelihood that the security forces will make contact with the terrorists,[1], and the initative remains with the terrorists. The military disadvantage of the security forces in this kind of conflict can be seen by comparing the fatalities on each side (Table 12). With the exception of Uruguay, where the Tupamaros deliberately avoided killing soldiers and police, the number of security force fatalities is more than double the number of terrorists killed. If accidental deaths are excluded the ratio becomes even more unfavorable to the security forces.[2]

A second set of tactics involves an attempt to catch the terrorists through extensive house searches in urban areas or sweeps of rural areas. In Uruguay, during August 1970, the police conducted over 20,000 house searches while, in January 1971, during "Operations Fan" in Montevideo more than 300,000 houses were searched by the army. Later the army mounted several operations in the rural departments of Tacuarembo, and Treinta y Tres. House searches were routine in Cyprus, and a series of "cordon and search" operations, involving thousands of soldiers, took place in the Troodos mountains and other areas where EOKA guerrillas were believed to be hiding. In Northern Ireland, according to official British Army statistics, 93,000 houses were searched during the

---

[1]D'Oliveira (1973) notes that in Uruguay "extensive patrolling...roadblocks and identification checks produced meagre results."

[2]It might be argued that terrorist organizations hide their dead or claim that they were innocent civilians for propaganda purposes. For example, in Cyprus the British claimed to have killed ninety EOKA and Paget thinks the true figure "was almost certainly higher" (1967:141). Given the strong emphasis upon the "heroic dead" in both EOKA and IRA ideology, this argument seems implausible.

TABLE 12   TERRORIST AND SECURITY FORCE FATALITIES

	Terrorist Fatalities	Security Force Fatalities	Ratio
EOKA (1955-58)	68	156	2.3
Tupamaros (1962-72)[1]	15	19	1.3
IRA (1970-80)	216	587	2.7
ETA (1975-81)	42	278	6.6
Italian Leftists (1977-81)	21	46	2.2

[1] Uruguay statistics up till April 15, 1972
when "State of Internal War" proclaimed

1970-80 period[1] and in the peak year of 1974,
19,600 houses were searched. Bell (1978:189) char-
acteristizes the policy of the Guardia Civil in
Spain as "sweeping searches, extensive arrests and
bloody shoot-outs." Indiscriminate mass searches
are not normal practice in Italy, but were used
after both the Moro and Dozier kidnappings.

Large-scale searches and other anti-terrorist
operations give the security forces the initiative
against the terrorists. However, since the security forces are operating in the dark as to the
identities and whereabouts of the terrorists these
massive operations usually result in very meagre
results at a high cost in military effort. For example, in Cyprus, one sweep lasting a week and involving 1700 troops produced only "two sacks of explosives, some rifles, pistols and daggers."
Another operation two months later in January, 1956
"captured the biggest quantity of arms to date including three machine-guns, a number of bombs,

[1]Boyle (1980:28) gives a significantly
higher figure for the number of houses searched
during this period.

hand-grenades and many small arms."[1] In Uruguay
according to d'Oliveira (1973) "dragnets by the
armed forces had few results."

For Northern Ireland monthly figures are
available for houses searched and for weapons
found; we can therefore plot the relationship
between the two. Table 13 shows how the success
rate falls dramatically as the number of houses
searched increases, with the varying success rate
reflecting the selectivity of the searches.

For obvious reasons we do not have reliable
quantitative data over time on all aspects of
security forcer activity. Information on such

TABLE 13   HOUSE SEARCHES AND WEAPON FINDS IN
NORTHERN IRELAND

Number of Houses Searched (monthly)	Weapons found/ 100 houses searched
2000+	4.5
1000-1999	8.2
300-999	8.8
200-299	13.5
100-199	30.7
less than 100	55.7

[1]Grivas was contemptuous of the British
tactics saying "one does not use a tank to catch
field mice--a cat will do the job better" (1965:71).
Paget (1967:168) compares the search for guerrillas
to "chasing individual fish in muddy and weedy
water with a very small net."

sensitive matters as interrogation procedures and surveillanced techniques is not available, for example. However, some data are available on military strength and non-routine actions, terrorists killed and terrorists arrested.

Security force actions could have either an immediate or a delayed impact. To see whether a particular type of action has an immediate impact we look at the correlations between terrorism and security force actions in the same month. To see whether there is a delayed effect, violence is lagged against security force activity for one through six months. Table 14, column 1, presents the correlations for the same month. The lagged correlations are shown, in column 2, only if they are negative and only for the months which show the best correlation.

It does not appear that troop strength or military activity, in itself, reduces terrorism immediately, and in fact military activity and terrorism are usually positively and significantly correlated. These results could be interpreted in two ways; either that military activity provokes terrorism or, more plausibly, that military activity is frequently a response to terrorism. The statistics do not suggest that military activity reduces terrorism in subsequent months. In only two cases do we find a negative lagged correlation, and in neither case is the correlation significant. Killing terrorists shows a similar pattern. Terrorists get killed in the months that terrorism is high and there is no indication of a later decline.

The relationship between arrests for terrorism and terrorist violence is more encouraging, and in several cases there are significant negative correlations. For example, in Nothern Ireland the higher the number of terrorists interned, the lower the level of violence. The same is true in Spain for ETA arrests, the more etarras arrested each month, the lower the level of violence. These results are interesting since they suggest that terrorist losses cannot be made up easily by recruiting new members.

	Same Month	Best Lag	Length of Lag
Cyprus			
Troop Strength	.39*		
Military Activity Index	.57*		
Curfews	.44*	-.09	
Terrorists killed	.59*	-.15	(5 months)
Terrorists captured	.56*	-.03	(5 months)
Terrorists convicted	.32*	-.01	(5 months)
Uruguay			
Military Activity Index	-.03	-.11	(5 months)
Terrorists captured	-.14	-.23*	(6 months)
Spain			
Terrorists killed	.04	-.04	(2 months)
Terrorist arrested	-.49*	-.49*	(2 months)
Italy			
Terrorists killed	.17	-.22	(4 months)
Terrorists arrested	-.15	-.12	(4 months)
Terrorists in jail	-.10	-.16	(4 months)
Northern Ireland (explosions)			
Troop strength	.53*		
Houses searched	.41*		
Terrorists killed	.49*		
Terrorists charged	.20*		
Terrorists interned	-.58*	-.73*	(3 months)
Northern Ireland (attacks on security forces)			
Troop strength	.56*		
Houses searched	.36*		
Terrorists killed	.73*		
Terrorists charged	.69*		
Terrorists interned	-.81*	-.80*	(2 months)
Northern Ireland (IRA killings)			
Troop strength	.59		
Houses searched	.39*		
Terrorists killed	.48*		
Terrorists interned	-.37*	-.33*	(1 month)

Note: Statistics shown are Pearsonian correlation coefficients. Lag
correlations only shown if negative. Starred if significant a
P< .05 level. A negative sign indicates that as the value of
the independent variable increases, terrorist violence decline

Summary of Research Findings

(1) Ceasefires are highly effective in reducing terrorism during the ceasefire period itself. Often violence stops completely, and on average the level of violence is only 16% of what it was in the period immediately preceding the truce. Protracted ceasefires appear to benefit the terrorists by allowing them to reorganize, with the result that after the truce violence resumes at a higher level. Short ceasefires, lasting less than a month, have no long-term effect on the level of violence.

(2) Many writers claim that terrorist violence can be reduced by improving economic conditions. However, an examination of the correlation between several economic indicators and violence levels does not support this view. Terrorism is rarely associated with rising unemployment or increases in the cost of living; instead it is more frequently linked to good economic conditions. This suggests that policies of general amelioration are not effective in reducing terrorism.

(3) In two cases, Northern Ireland and the Basque provinces of Spain, the government tried to reduce popular support for the terrorists by making extensive reforms. The consequences of these reform programs are complex. Two phases of the process; the initial announcement of concessions and the formulation of specific policies stimulate terrorist violence. The data suggest that reforms were eventually followed by a decline in the level of violence. One should note, however, that even after significant changes have been made in Northern Ireland and the Basque provinces, terrorism still remains a major problem in both areas.

(4) In attempting to reduce popular support for terrorism, governments usually rely more upon the carrot than the stick. However, in Cyprus collective punishments (fines, property seizures and shop closures) were employed against towns with a record of terrorist activity. The punishments appear to reduce violence in those areas where they were imposed. This reduction is most marked after the first punishment, but subsequent punishments have less effect or increase violence.

(5)   States typically respond to a terrorist
threat by enacting emergency legislation which de-
prives the population of various civil liberties.
There is a basic similarity in the emergency powers
adopted in the cases considered: detention without
trial, house searches without warrants, special
courts for suspected terrorists, etc.   No relation
is discernible between the imposition of such powers and the subsequent level of terrorist activity;
nor does terrorism decline as the emergency legislation is made more severe.   Emergency legislation
may be justified, however, both as a symbol of
government determination and as a framework wherein
the security forces may operate effectively.

(6)   Another response to terrorism is to increase the size of the security forces and upgrade
their capabilities through training and administrative reorganization. The two most common counter-
insurgency tactics, patrolling and indiscriminate
mass searches, produce only meagre results.   Security force activity, such as searching houses, is
highly correlated with, and presumably a response
to, terrorist violence.   There is no indication
from our data that security force activity in one
month reduces terrorism in subsequent months.   However, in Northern Ireland and Spain, there is a relationship between the number of suspected terrorists in prison and the level of violence; the more
terrorists imprisoned the lower the violence level.

The Simultaneous Effect of Several Policies: Multiple Regression Analysis.

Our analysis up to this point has implicitly adopted a ceteris paribus assumption, and looked at each policy and its impact as though it operated in isolation. In reality, of course, several policies are often applied at the same time; reforms are made while houses are being searched, unemployment declines while martial law is imposed. This mix of policies creates some difficulties in imputing causality. If violence declines during a period when reforms are granted and large numbers of houses are searched, which policy is responsible for the decline?

To see if any different relationships would appear if we considered the simultaneous effect of several policies, we carried out a multiple regression analysis. The full results are presented in appendix 2. Seven equations, three for Northern Ireland and one for each of the other countries are shown.

Each equation includes variables for military activity, terrorist arrests, terrorist fatalities and economic conditions. Dummy variables for truces and reforms were also entered into the equations where appropriate. Unfortunately some variables could not be included because data were missing for too many months.

Generally the results of the multiple regression analysis support the conclusions that we came to, on the basis of simple correlations, or before-and-after comparisons. Usually, good economic conditions are not linked to lower levels of violence. Military activity and terrorist violence are strongly associated. An examination of the association between specific military actions and types of terrorist violence in Northern Ireland shows that the strongest links are between the security forces opening fire and being fired on, and between explosions and IRA terrorists being killed. Presumably this reflects the fact that soldiers

90

return fire when attacked, and that many IRA terrorists blow themselves up with their own bombs.

Some of the equations do suggest different conclusions as to the effect of certain policies. First, there is a significant positive relationship between unemployment and IRA killings (i.e. IRA killings increase during periods of high unemployment). Second, during the existence of the "No-Go" areas in Northern Ireland, violence was higher than it was after the British Army moved into them.[1] This finding may be interpreted in various ways. One interpretation might be that, although military activity does not reduce violence, doing nothing is an even worse policy. Third, reforms did not reduce violence in Northern Ireland, although there is some evidence that they had an impact in Spain. It is possible that more advanced statistical models, such as interrupted time-series analysis, and other regression models that correct for auto-correlation, would reveal different relationships among the variables.

---

[1]"No-Go" areas were established in the Catholic areas by the IRA in 1969. The British Army and the RUC did not enter them until after Operation Motorman on July 31, 1972.

CHAPTER 4

DISCUSSION

It would be satisfying to report that we had
identified a number of policies that were consis-
tently successful in reducing terrorism, but such
is not the case. Instead what our research suggests is that some policies do not work at all, and
some policies are successful in certain situations
but not in others.

Overall the authorities were most successful
in eradicating terrorism in Uruguay and Italy. In
Uruguay, the Tupamaros were completely destroyed in
1972, and in Italy, although remnants of the Red
Brigades still exist, there has been only sporadic
activity since 1982. The nationalist groups, ETA
and IRA, have proved more difficult to control.
The current level of violence is much lower than in
the past, but still significant.[1] From a political
viewpoint both groups have been partially successful. IRA terrorism creates a situation in which
British withdrawal is a strong possibility. ETA
terrorism was a major factor in the Spanish decision to grant autonomy to the Basque provinces. The
British were the losers in the Cyprus insurgency,
although EOKA failed to achieve their goal of enosis. Instead in 1960 the island became independent, under a constitution that guaranteed the
Turkish minority a privileged political position.

In this final chapter we relate our research
findings to the general literature on terrorism,
and speculate on how they can be explained by existing theories. Terrorism is carried out by
organized groups, whose leaders have certain political goals which they hope to achieve by engaging
in terrorism. In order to mount and maintain a
campaign, the terrorist organization needs men,
supplies and a degree of popular support. Therefore a successful anti-terrorist policy must lead
to a reduction in one or more of these factors. In

---

[1]Fatalities in Northern Ireland show a
decline from a high of 467 in 1972 to 97 in 1982,
while in the Basque provinces the decline was from
65 in 1979 to 31 in 1981.

explaining why some policies fail to work or are counterproductive, two things should be born in mind; that policies often have unintended consequences and that several policies applied simultaneously can work at cross-purposes.

Societies threatened with terrorism usually respond by becoming increasingly repressive. Military and police actions become more extensive, and are less subject to legal controls. However, the degree of repression varies significantly among countries, and over time within each country. More importantly, repression can be applied selectively or indiscriminately, and with varying safeguards for the civil liberties of the general population.

At a certain level, repression is undeniably effective. A regime which is willing to arrest, torture and kill enough of its citizens will quickly uncover most terrorist organizations. If punishments are sufficiently severe and ruthlessly applied to those suspected of being supporters, then the number willing to help the terrorists will decline rapidly. There is consensus that the destruction of the Tupamaros was due to the harsh policies employed by the army. D'Oliveira (1973) talks of how "energetic and professional interrogation...started to pay dividends," while Porzecanski (1973), Labrousse (1973) and Handelman (1978) less euphemistically stress mass arrests and torture. Of the cases examined, Uruguay was the only one in which the regime resorted to such extreme measures, but other examples such as Argentina could be used to make the same point.[1]

However, although military dictatorships can suppress terrorism using extreme measures, there is no evidence that, short of this point, repression is an effective strategy. Whether we measure repression in terms of the deprivation of

---

[1]For an account of how the Montoneros and other leftists were crushed by the Argentine military, see Gillespie (1982:244-252). Gillespie cites estimates that 10,000 were killed, 15,000 imprisoned and 30,000 "disappeared." A majority of those killed and tortured were merely suspected of being Montonero sympathizers.

civil liberties, the size of the security forces, the amount of military activity or the number of people killed by the security forces, the more repressive regimes are no more successful in reducing terrorism than the more liberal regimes. Increasing repression did not lower the level of terrorist violence in Cyprus, Spain, Northern Ireland or Italy.

This is a very significant negative finding which can be explained by considering the impact of repressive policies upon the general population. Although the purpose of military activity may be to capture terrorists and discover hidden weapons, the life of the civilian population is directly affected. MacStiofain (1975:216) says that in the republican areas of Belfast "during periods of particular pressure on certain districts, the same home would be searched daily for a week, and even three or four times a day. Outside in the street...morning searches of pedestrians and vehicles made people late for work...(while foot patrols walked) all over the little gardens, peering through windows." An American, living in a small Catholic village, describes how during army searches of cars and buses "no one is above suspicion and no one is trusted, compounding impersonal intimidation with personal affront," (Bufwach, 1982:135). Measures such as these are intrinsically intrusive and alienating, even if soldiers and police behave correctly and courteously, which is not always the case. MacStiofain, for example, charges that British troops were routinely abusive and brutal to the Catholics (1975:215-7). In Uruguay "the population was incensed by the continual police controls...doors were broken down...and things were stolen," (Labrousse, 1973:130). It must be concluded therefore that heavy-handed repression is counterproductive, and should not be used routinely, but only for short periods in times of extreme emergency.

As an alternative to military measures, some writers have argued for a strategy aimed at reducing popular support for the terrorists by improving economic conditions and making reforms.

"To pursue Mao Tse-Tung's simile...the policy must be to destroy the fish...by draining the pond rather than by chasing individual fish with a very small net." (Paget, 1967:168)

Our findings do not support this position. The level of terrorist violence does not decline during prosperous times. Neither in Spain nor in Northern Ireland did reforms have a noticeable impact. These disappointing results can be explained in one of three ways. First it is possible that terrorists can function without much popular support. This might explain the Uruguayan and Italian results, where the terrorists seem to have relied upon urban anonymity rather than support from a friendly population. However, the explanation seems implausible given the nature of the campaigns in Cyprus, Northern Ireland and the Basque provinces. In these areas many people know who the terrorists are, and terrorist actions are often carried out with the connivance and assistance of the local population. A second explanation is more likely; those who support the terrorists do so because of ethnic solidarity or ideological commitment, which are unlikely to be affected by modest changes in their economic situation. It has been argued that the reforms in Northern Ireland and the Basque provinces did not go far enough, and were not really meaningful. However, it is difficult to see what more could have been done, given economic and political constraints. For example, full employment through Northern Ireland might lead to Catholic acceptance of the status quo, but the massive amount of economic aid that this would require is not likely to be forthcoming from a recession-wracked United Kingdom. A third explanation for the lack of impact of reforms and economic conditions is that their effect is overriden by other factors. Once terrorism reaches a certain level the daily life of the civilian population is significantly affected by both the terrorism itself and the

countermeasures taken by the security forces.[1] The
population may turn against the terrorists because
of the atrocities they commit, or protect them because the security forces behave in a brutal or
partisan fashion. However, they are unlikely to
pay much attention to reforms, when faced with a
variety of life-threatening situations.

The most desirable policy is one which results
in the capture of terrorists without the general
population being subjected to constant harrassment
by the military. A policy of vigorously seeking
out terrorists can be advocated on several grounds.
Terrorist violence is organized violence, as shown
by the ability of the terrorist leaders to halt
their campaign when it serves their interests to do
so. The active terrorists are few in number, so
therefore if a significant proportion can be captured the organization will be crippled or destroyed. Furthermore, the punishment of captured terrorists may deter potential recruits.

These arguments are partly supported by our
study. In both Northern Ireland and Spain we found
that the more terrorists in jail, the lower the
level of violence. We can only speculate why no
such relationship is found in the other countries.
Possibly the number of arrests may be too low to
affect the operational capabilities of the terrorist organization. Alternatively the official statistics may be misleading, and include as "terrorists" many who are merely passive supporters or
political dissidents. A further possibility is

---

[1]In Northern Ireland, a 1973 survey found
that 23% reported that they or some member of
their family had suffered a property loss, and 10%
a personal injury.

that terrorist losses can be made up by new recruits.[1]

Good intelligence is crucial to identifying and capturing terrorists. Unfortunately normal criminal investigation procedures are largely ineffective due to the lack of any personal connection between the terrorists and their victims, the cell structure of the terrorist organization and public sympathy for, or fear of, the terrorists.

The interrogation of suspects or captured terrorists is an obvious source of information, but it is difficult to draw the line between acceptable and unacceptable forms of interrogation. In every case, except Italy,[2] there is evidence that the security forces used methods that involved brutality and torture. A committee of the Uruguayan Senate concluded in June 1970 that the police routinely used electric shock, beatings, burns, and starvation to gather information. When the armed forces took over from the police, in April 1972, interrogation became:

> "much more prolonged, systematic, and sophisticated. For instance, suspected Tupamaro collaborators were said to be subjected to a routine consisting of, perhaps, two days of

---

[1]In Cyprus the military skills of most EOKA recruits were minimal and the majority had never handled automatic weapons prior to joining. Grivas, the EOKA leader, noted that "losses did not weaken the organization for the gaps were quickly filled by young fighters from the ranks" (1965:34). Although the Spanish authorities detained a number equal to the entire ETA membership during 1978-81, the organization was able to survive because many detainees were released after a short period, and new members were recruited (Clark 1984:263).

[2]In Italy, there were occasional claims by the terrorists or their lawyers that suspects were beaten up, made to drink salt walter, etc., but it has never been alleged that such procedures were officially sanctioned.

<u>planton</u> (prolonged standing without food),
a week of <u>capucha</u> (completely blindfolded
imprisonment), and a few mornings of <u>sub-marinos</u> (immersion of the prisoner's <u>head</u> in
water, up to the point of asphyxiation, every
half hour or so)...Forms of psychological torture (such as interruption of sleep, with-
holding food or drink, and threats) and drug-
induced confessions were also frequently reported" (Porzecanski, 1973:68).

At least one prisoner died under torture, and
two others were paralyzed. In Cyprus, EOKA
suspects were frequently beaten by British inter-
rogators, and Papchrysostomou (1969) lists nine
who "died under interrogation." In Northern Ireland interrogation procedures have been criticized
on several grounds. Beginning in August 1971 there
were complaints, confirmed by the Compton Committee
in November 1971, of what was called "interrogation
in depth." For up to five days, suspects were hood-
ed, subjected to continuous monotonous noise,
forced to stand against the wall supporting themselves on their hands, and deprived of food and
sleep. These techniques were taught to the RUC by
the British army, and were apparently authorized at
the highest levels. The European Human Rights
Court decided in January 1978 that the procedures
constituted "inhumane treatment", and that the
United Kingdom, by their use had violated article
III of the European Human Rights Convention. Interrogation in depth was abandoned in March 1972,
but from 1977 onwards, complaints began to be made
about beatings of suspects during interrogation.
In response to these complaints, a number of
reforms were made in mid-1979. Throughout the
Franco period, there were frequent reports of brutal interrogation and torture of Basque nationalists. Amnesty International concluded that, in 1975
during the state of Exception in the Basque provinces, at least 295 people were tortured, some re-
peatedly. The methods of torture included:

"severe and systematic beatings with a variety
of contusive weapons, falanga (beating on the
soles of the feet), buring with cigarettes,
near drownings by being submerged in water
while suspended upside-down, enforced sleep-
lessness, and forms of psychological stress,
including mock executions and sexual threats."

98

By 1978 torture was much reduced but there were "enough signs of its continued use to ...concern the families of Basques in prison" and former ETA members were "routinely detained and interogated, sometimes for several days" (Clark, 1979:369-371).

In Northern Ireland, the British Army maintained a dossier on the whole population in the hard-core Republican areas, through various mass surveillance techniques.[1] Army sources stress the use of foot patrols and observation points, but according to Boyle (1980:26) "the principle mechanisms were regular house searches (and)... frequent arrests and screening of the population." The disadvantage of the system is that large numbers of innocent people must be placed under surveillance, arrested and questioned. The method of obtaining intelligence through mass surveillance techniques was only used in Northern Ireland, and discontinued after 1974.[2]

Paying informants is another standard method of obtaining intelligence. In Uruguay, high rewards were offered for information leading to the rescue of kidnap victims, or the arrest and conviction of a Tupamaro. For the former, the rewards ranged from $20,000 to $90,000 while for the latter, they were set at $8,000. However, according

---

[1]"Some observers reckon that up to 40% of the population...is on record" in the central filing system maintained at Army headquarters. The files contain "detailed descriptions and assessments of movements and associates. It is highly efficient." Fortnight, 7/5/74.

[2]Undercover units are probably still operating On one occasion the army operated a laundry, which made collections and deliveries in Catholic areas. Laundry was tested for traces of explosives, gun oil, etc.

to Porzecanski (1973:62) none of these rewards were ever collected.[1] In Cyprus, the British relied heavily on paid informers, and most captures of EOKA terrorists resulted from information obtained in this fashion. The informers were highly-paid; one received £200, the equivalent of a year's wages, for revealing the names of those in an EOKA cell. In Northern Ireland the use of paid informers is generally acknowledged, but until recently British army officers complained that they were unable to offer potential informers legal indemnity or much money (Evelegh, 1978:68-75). At the end of 1981, however, the use of "supergrasses" began. A supergrass is a convicted terrorist, who testifies against his former comrades in return for a reduced prison sentence or freedom with a new identity. As of August 1983, 31 supergrasses had given information leading to the arrest of nearly 300 suspects. Official sources give the program credit for a significant decline in terrorist violence in 1983[1]

In Italy, intelligence gathering was originally restricted by various regulations, (Pisano, 1979:146-7), Blackstone, 1978:105). However in 1980 a law was passed which empowered the government to halve the sentences of those convicted of terrorism if they cooperated with the police by providing information. So-called "pentitos" (penitents) have provided information which led to the arrest and conviction of many terrorists. In a report to the Italian Chamber of Deputies, Prime Minister Craxi cited the clemency law as a major factor in the decline of terrorism.[2]

---

[1]See Irish Times 4/21/83, Washington Post 8/14/83, and New York Times 9/29/83, for discussions of the program. Eight defectors were killed by IRA and INLA and others retracted their testimony following threats to their families.

[2]See New York Times 12/17/84. The first pentito was Patricio Peci in 1981. Each new wave of arrests results in more pentitos, which leads to more arrests and so on. For example, in a series of trials in July-August 1983, 99 terrorists were convicted on evidence supplied by terrorists captured after the Dozier kidnapping.

It is certain that terrorism will be a problem in some societies for many years and our study suggests that current remedies will be only partially successful. The most effective anti-terrorist strategy is likely to be one that uses a mix of policies appropriate to the specific national situation, and coordinated with one another. Even then a quick and easy victory in the war against terrorism is unlikely.

DATA SOURCES AND CODING PROCEDURES

The data used in this study will be discussed under three headings; terrorist violence and security force countermeasures, economic conditions, significant events.

Terrorist Violence and Security Force Countermeasures.

The Uruguay Data

The main source for Tupamaro actions, and security force countermeasures, is a 63 page chronology, in Spanish, by Mayans (1971). Mayans' history is itself derived, in part, from two other chronologies; that of Mercador and Vera (1969) and that found in Tricontinental (March-April, 1970). Mayans' study is described by one expert on Latin American terrorism as "the most complete single volume compilation of documentary materials relating to the Tupamaro movement...the best reference work available today in English or Spanish" (Russell, 1974:73). Unfortunately the chronology only goes up to March 1971 (i.e., to the point at which a state of internal war was declared). For the two year period following, during which the Tupamaros were crushed by the army, the sources are Litt and Kohl's chronology (1974) which runs from June 1962 through July 1973, a report by the Uruguayan Ministry of the Interior covering seven months in 1972 and material from Keesings.

Since information on security force activity was not given in a quantified form it was necessary to create "an index of military activity" by scoring each reported operation. Large operations and searches were scored 10 points, small operations 1 point. How well our sources report the Tupamaro violence and government countermeasures is difficult to assess, since the government exercised censorship over press reports of the conflict. One figure is known, however, and can be used to estimate the degree of coverage. According to Porzecanski (1973:28), 648 Tupamaros were captured from December 1966 through June

1972, while our count for a slightly shorter period, January 1968 to June 1972, is 606. This suggests that, during this period, our sources record almost all the activity. After the state of internal war was declared in April 15, 1972, the figures are less reliable, although the Uruguayan government issued statistics on the total number of terrorists arrested, weapons found, houses searched and bases discovered on May 15, June 15, and July 15, 1972.

The Cyprus Data

The data on the Cyprus conflict are extensive, and can be classified as either anti or pro-EOKA. Each category, by itself, is partisan and incomplete; put together a rich data set is created. Information on terrorist activity and security force countermeasures comes from several sources. Official records are available on curfews, since each curfew order had to be approved by the governor, and they are all published, along with information on place and date, in the Cyprus Gazette. Killings by EOKA are given in the official casualty list, and are broken down by month, by ethnicity and by victim characteristics (soldier, police or civilian). Keesings gives a chronology of "terrorist activities together with counter-operations by the security forces." The Keesings chronology is limited to "major" incidents but is very useful because it notes their location. Some additional information can be found in Kosut (1970) and Blaxland (1971). Blaxland's account is derived in part from regimental sources. All the above give the official British view of the insurgency and appear to be based to a large extent upon press releases by the Cyprus government or British army. Fortunately, the insurgent version is well recorded in Papachrysostomou's work, "The Archives of the Fallen" (1969). As its title suggests, this is a hagiology of those who died in the liberation struggle, listing the dead under six categories (e.g., EOKA killed in action, EOKA executed by the British, etc.). The date of death is given in all except two cases. In a separate publication, Papachrysostomou (1977) lists every Greek Cypriot who was imprisoned, the charge, date of trial and sentence.

The statistics on British troop strength are derived from Blaxland, whose account of the campaign details the movements of British army units into and out of the island. By combining the information in Blaxland with various totals for particular dates given in Grivas (1965) Foley and Scobie (1975) etc., it is possible to estimate the changes in monthly troop strength throughout the period. Since Cyprus was used as a base during the Suez crisis of November 1956, and again in mid-1958, the total number of troops on the island is not always a valid indicator of the number of troops available for anti-EOKA operations. Those units which merely passed through the island without taking part in anti-EOKA operations are not included in the monthly totals.

Information on military activity is available for non-routine operations, and usually the number of troops and the area involved is given. For example, the military announced November 7, 1955 that "a large scale operation in the mountains east of Kyrenia...in which 1,700 troops took part" had taken place the previous week. An "index of military activity" was constructed by scoring each operation. An operation described as "large," involving more than 1,000 troops or a sweep of an extensive area such as the Troodos mountains was scored 10. An operation in a town, or involving 500-1,000 troops scored 5. A search of a village or section of a town scored 2, and a search of a particular building scored 1. All operations in a particular month were summed. Keesings and Blaxland usually report the number of terrorists and suspects captured in each operation, as well as the number of weapons found. For example, an operation in October 1956 "ended after 31 EOKA terrorists had been captured, over 50 suspects held and large stores of arms seized." The distinction between "terrorists" and "suspects" is apparently based upon the evidence against them and is linked to their subsequent treatment. Terrorists were those who had a price on their head, caught committing a terrorists act, or with weapons in their possession. They were usually prosecuted in regular court. Suspected sympathizers, whose involvement in EOKA was more difficult to prove, were usually detained without trial. The total number of arrested

or captured terrorists given in Keesings agrees
closely with the annual Cyprus police reports
(1955-1959) and Papachrysostomou (1977).

The Northern Irish Data

The fatalities associated with the Northern
Irish conflict are, for the most part, well-docu-
mented. Our death file has been created by combining several sources, cross checking them
against one another and, if possible, finding any
information still missing.

The records kept by the Royal Ulster Constabulary (RUC) are the basic source for Northern
Irish fatalities. The RUC records generally give
the name, age, address, where a person was killed
and the cause of death (i.e., gun shot wounds,
explosion, etc.). Unfortunately, the records usually do not provide information on the victim's
religion, whether or not the victim was a member
of a terrorist organization, or by whom the person was killed. Thus, it is not possible to distinguish between, for example, people shot by the
army or those assassinated by terrorists. Fortunately the files maintained by the Belfast
Office of the Irish Times while based upon the
RUC files, provide additional information as to
the circumstances surrounding a death, the likely
killer and the characteristics of the victim. The
RUC/Irish Times records do not begin until October, 1971. For deaths prior to this date there
are two sources. The Belfast Newsletter (September 8, 1971) lists the first 100 deaths, giving
name, age, address and a brief characterization
of the cause of death. A written answer to a
question in the House of Commons (26 October,
1971:56-70) gives the name, age, occupation,
place where killed, date and cause of death for
the first 100 victims in 1971.

Deutsch and Magowan's chronology (1974) records on a daily basis all the significant events
that took place in Northern Ireland from 1968
through 1973. While rarely identifying fatalities by name, the chronology mentions about 90%.
A typical entry might note that "a twenty year
old girl was shot dead as she waited for a bus on

the Crumlin Road when shots were fired at soldiers on patrol." McKeown (1972) lists the first
500 deaths by name and classifies them into six
categories; members of the security forces, terrorists, victims of terrorist activity, those
shot by the security forces, assassinations and
those killed during rioting. Assassinations have
been studied in great detail by Dillon and Lehane
(1973). The Last Post (1976) gives the names of
all the Provisional IRA who died in action
through the period. Since the book is published
by the National Graves Commission, a Republican
organization closely linked to the Provisional
IRA, the list is virtually a definitive honor
roll of the Provisional IRA.

The British army keeps excellent records on
violence and security force counter-measures including monthly statistics on explosions, incidents in which the security forces were fired
upon, incidents in which the security forces
opened fire, houses searched, weapons found,
arrests for terrorist offenses and army force
levels. From February 1973 to December 1975, the
army recorded a statistic "terrorists out of action" which refers to the total number interned
at the end of each month. Beginning January
1976, when internment was ended, this was replaced by a category "charges for terrorist offenses." The "weapons found" and "terrorists
out of action" categories are broken down by religion.

The Spanish Data

The Spanish authorities do not release detailed information on terrorism nor on
counter-insurgency operations. In order to con-
struct a data set of ETA-related fatalities, the
sources used were Equipo Cinco (1977), which lists
the victims from November 1975 to February 1977,
Keesings, The London Times and The New York
Times. For the period after January 1980, the U.
S. Consulate in Bilbao, provided information on
terrorist incidents in the Basque region, based
on local newspaper reports. Professor Robert
Clark, George Mason University, has developed a
data-set of ETA attacks. While Clark has collected much more information on woundings and

106

kidnappings, our statistics on ETA killings are fairly similar overall. For the 1975-1980 period, Clark found 250 killings while our sources list 243. Since Clark has more information on victim characteristics and why the person was killed , the information on ETA victims in Chapter 2, Table 2 is taken from one of his papers (Clark, 1981).

No official figures of the number of Basque political prisoners are available on a regular monthly basis. However, a variety of sources (Clark, 1979, Keesings, etc.) give such figures for certain dates. For example, Clark reports that there were 150 Basque prisoners in November 1976 and 103 in March 1977 while Keesings notes that the total number of political prisoners (Basque and other) was 636 in July 1976 and 170 in March 1977. Keesings also records the arrests and trials of a large number of etarras and other Basque nationalists. These data have been used to estimate the number of Basque political prisoners for each month. In making the estimates it was assumed 1) that Basque and non-Basques were released at the same rate under the various amnesties, 2) that the rate of increase between two dates corresponds to the number of arrests and 3) that any remaining values can be calculated by simple interpolation.

The Italian Data

The statistics on Italian terrorism are acknowledged to be somewhat unreliable. According to one Italian expert (Anonymous, 1978:159) the statistics "include in the same category heterogeneous events and events not reliably identifiable as terrorist." It should be noted that different writers give different figures as to the number of terrorist attacks in a particular year. (Thus for 1977, Ronchey (1979) gives a total of 2,128 attacks, Pisano (1979) 2,127 and the PCI 2,013 in one report and 2,124 in another). Another problem is that the official statistics include acts of widely varying severity, minor acts of vandalism as well as homicides and kidnappings.

This study used data from five sources; the
Ministry of the Interior, the PCI (Sezione prob-
lemi dello Stato), Pisano (1979), Galleni (1981)
and various English language newspapers (New
York Times, London Times, and Keesings). The
most detailed information is found in the annual
and semiannual reports put out by the PCI. These
list those killed and wounded in terrorist
attacks and give the name, victim characteristics, place of attack and group responsible. One
might be suspicious of information provided by
the PCI, but a comparison between the PCI data
and that from other sources does not reveal any
obvious bias or omissions. In 1977 for example,
the PCI data yield a total of 8 killed and 36
wounded in terrorist attacks, the other sources
combined 8 and 42. The PCI statistics also a-
gree closely with the other sources as to the
targets of the attacks. The measure of terrorist
activity used in this study is the total number
killed and wounded plus other shooting incidents
and kidnappings reported in any of the above
sources.

The New York Times, London Times, Keesings
and Pisano are the source for terrorist captures
and arrests. Figures of the total number of terrorists in jail are given irregularly and are usually broken down by organization (Red Brigade,
Front Line, etc). Between these dates it was
assumed that changes in the jail population cor-
responded to the rate of arrests.

Economic Conditions

The best single source on economic conditions
is the United Nations' "Monthly Bulletin of Statistics" which was used to obtain unemployment
and cost of living data for Spain and Italy, and
cost of living data for Uruguay. The Northern
Irish unemployment statistics up to September
1977 are from the Northern Ireland Department of
Finance, "Digest of Statistics". For the period
since then the figures were provided by the Department of Manpower Services, Belfast. Uruguay
was one of the most economically developed and
socially progressive societies in Latin America,

and a wealth of information on economic conditions is available in the publications of the Instituto de Estudios Politicos (1965), the Instituto de Economia (1973) and Banco de la Republica
Oriental del Uruguay (1967). Statistics on unemployment were supplied privately by the Direccion
General de Estadistica y Censos. The annual publications of the Department of Labour and the Financial Secretary's Office were the source for
unemployment and cost of living data for Cyprus.
When the base year for the index changed, the -
figures were recalculated to make the series con-
sistent. For gaps of one or two months, the
missing values were estimated by simple interpolation. The reader should note that the Spanish
data are for the whole country not just the Basque provinces.

Significant Events

For information on truces, emergency powers,
anti-terrorist legislation, reforms and other
significant events the main source was Keesings.
In addition other sources were for Cyprus, Crawshaw (1978), for Uruguay, Mayans (1971), Litt and
Kohl (1974), and Porzecanski (1973), for Northern
Ireland, Rose (1976), Darby (1976), Boyle (1975,
1980), Deutsch and Magowan (1974), Wilkinson
(1977), and Holland (1981), for Spain, Clark
(1979), and for Italy, Pisano (1979), and Bell
(1978).

If there were contradictions between different sources the more detailed account was used.
For example, Porzecanski (1973:59) says that one
Tupamaro truce began September 6, 1971 and "lasted for five months" (i.e., it presumably ended in
February, 1972). However, Keesings describes the
truce as ending on January 6, 1972 when "the Tupamaros took over a radio station and announced
the end of the ceasefire," so the latter, more
precise, source was used.

Appendix 2

MULTIPLE REGRESSION ANALYSIS

Equation 1		Cyprus: EOKA killings
Variable	Unstandardized Regression Coefficient	Beta Weight
Terrorists captured	.128	.12
Consumer Price Index	-.558	-.01
Unemployed	.787	.06
Curfews	.330	.01
Terrorists killed	.143*	.38
Military Activity Index	.521*	.44
(Constant)	.229	

n = 46   Adjusted R^2 = .44   F = 6.79*

* P < .05

Equation 2	Uruguay: All Terrorist Incidents	

Variable	Unstandardized Regression Coefficients	Beta Weight
Terrorists captured	.948	.08
Public Sector Incomes	.239*	.43
Unemployment	-.515*	-.20
Truces	-.597*	-.38
Military Activity Index	.981	
(Constant)	-.103	
n = 52	Adjusted R^2 = .25	F = 4.27*

Equation 3   Northern Ireland:Security Forces Fired Upon.

Variable	Unstandardized Regression Coefficient	Beta Weight
No Go Areas abolished	-.859*	-.18
Houses Searched	.306*	.09
Security Forces open fire	.547*	.95
Truces	.473*	.08
Unemployment	.127	.01
IRA killed	.424	.01
RFeforms	.549*	.13
(Constant)	.246	

n = 119   Adjusted R^2 = .93   F =- 221.10*

Equation 4   Northern Ireland: Explosions

Variable	Unstandardized Reregression Coefficient	Beta Weight
No Go Areas abolished	-.241*	-.26
Houses Searched	.189*	.29
Security Forces open fire	.398*	.34
Truces	.115	.01
Unemployment	.768	.03
IRA killed	.557*	.31
Reforms	.133	.16
(Constant)	.389	

n = 119   Adjusted R^2 = .47   F= 16.05*

Equation 5	Northern Ireland: Killings by IRA.	

Variable	Unstandardizedd Regression Coefficient	Beta Weight
No Go Areas abolished	-.184	-.11
Houses Searched	.324*	.29
Security Forces open fire	.933*	.47
Truces	.568*	.30
Unemployment	.113*	.23
IRA killed	.547*	.18
Reforms	.193	.13
(Constant)	-.334	

$n = 119$ Adjusted $R^2 = .52$ $F = 19.11$*

Variable	Unstandardized Regression Coefficient	Beta Weight
Reform	-.22	- .28
Terrorists killed	.321	.09
Consumer Price Index	-.770	-1.88
Unemployment	.170	1.76
Truces	.142	- .10
Arrests	-.227*	- .93
(Constant	.192	

Equation 6   Spain: ETA killings

$n = 37$ Adjusted R^2 = .41   F = 4.97*

Equation 7	Italy: Terrorist Incidents	
Variable	Unstandardized Regression Coefficient	Beta Weight
Terrorists Arrested	-.163	-.06
Unemployment	-.506	-.11
Consumer Price Index	-.231	-.03
Terrorists Killed	.820	.15
(Constant)	.143	

n = 53   Adjusted R^2 = .03   F= .67

BIBLIOGRAPHY

Amnesty International. Report of an Amnesty
    International Mission to Spain. London, 1975

Anonymous. (Described as "in the forefront of
    controlling terrorism in Italy."). "Phen-
    omenological and Dynamic Aspects of Terrorism
    in Italy," Terrorism: An International
    Journal, 2 (1978): 159-168.

Banco do la Republica Oriental del Uruguay.
    Boletin Estadistico. Montevideo, 1967.

Bell, J. Bowyer. A Time of Terror. New York:
    Basic Books, 1978.

_____. The Secret Army: A History of the
    IRA 1916-79. Cambridge:MIT Press, 1979.

Blackstone Associates. Risk Assessment for
    Italy. Washington, D.C., 1978.

Blaxland, Gregory. The Regiments Depart: A His-
    tory of the British Army. London:Kimber,
    1971.

Boyle, Kevin. Law and State. University of
    Massachusetts Press, 1975.

_____. Ten Years on in Northern Ireland:
    The Legal Control of Political Violence.
    Nottingham:Cobden Trust, 1980.

Bufwach, Mary. Village without Violence.
    Cambridge: Schenkman, 1982.

Cameron Commission. Disturbances in Northern
    Ireland: Report of the Cameron Commission.
    Cmd. 532, 1969.

Clark, Robert. The Basques: The Franco Years
    and Beyond. Reno: University of Nevada
    Press, 1979.

_____. Patterns of Insurgent Violence in Spain's Basque Provinces," Southwestern Political Science Association Meeting (March 1981).

_____. "The Roots of Insurgency: The Social Origins of ETA," International Studies Association Meeting (October 1981).

Clark, Robert. The Basque Insurgents: ETA, 1952-80. Madison: University of Wisconsin Press, 1984.

Clutterbuck, Richard. Guerrillas and Terrorists. Ohio University Press, 1980.

Crawshaw, Nancy. The Cyprus Revolt. London: George Allen and Unwin, 1978.

Cyprus. Department of Labour. Annual Report. Nicosia.

Cyprus. Financial Secretary's Office. Statistics Section. Statistical Abstract. Nicosia.

Cyprus Government. The Cyprus Gazette. Nicosia (Monthly).

Cyprus Police. Annual Report. Nicosia.

Darby, John. Conflict in Northern Ireland. New York:Barnes and Noble, 1976.

Deutsch, Richard and Magowan, Vivien. Northern Ireland: A Chronology of Events. Belfast: Blackstaff Press, 1974.

Dillon, Martin and Lehane, Denis. Political Murder in Northern Ireland. Harmondsworth: Penguin, 1973.

D'Oliviera, Sergio. "Uruguay and the Tupamaro Myth," Military Review, 53 (April 1973): 25-36.

Equipo Cinco. Las Victimas del Post Franquismo. Madrid:Sedmay, 1977.

Evelegh, Robin. *Peacekeeping in a Democratic Society*. London: Hurst and Company, 1978.

Fisk, Robert. *The Point of No Return*. London: Times Books, 1975.

Foley, Charles and Scobie, W.I. *The Struggle for Cyprus*. Stanford: Hoover Institution Press, 1975.

Galleni, Mauro. *Rapporto sul Terrorismo*. Milano:Rizzoli, 1981.

Gillespie, Richard. *Soldiers of Peron*. Oxford: Clarlendon Press, 1982.

Grivas, George. *Guerrilla Warfare and EOKA's Struggle*. London:Longmans, 1964.

_____. *Memoirs*. New York:Praeger, 1965.

Gurr, Ted Robert. *Why Men Rebel*. Princeton: Princeton University Press, 1970.

Halperin, Ernst. *Terrorism in Latin America*. Beverly Hills, Calif:Sage Publications, 1976.

Handelman, Howard. "Military Authoritarianism and Political Change in Uruguay," *American University Field Service Reports*, 27 (1978).

Hewitt, Christopher. "Catholic Grievances, Catholic Nationalism and Violence in Northern Ireland during the Civil Rights Period." *British Journal of Sociology*, 32 (September 1981):362-380.

Holland, Jack. *Too Long a Sacrifice*. New York:Dodd, Mead and Company, 1981.

Instituto de Economia. *Estudios y Coyuntura*. Montevideo, 1973.

Instituto de Estudios Politicos. *Uruguay*. Montevideo, 1965.

Katz, Robert. *Days of Wrath*. New York:Double-day and Company, 1980.

<u>Keesing's Contemporary Archives</u>. (Weekly).

Kohl, James and Litt, John. <u>Urban Guerrilla Warfare in Latin America</u>. Cambridge:MIT Press, 1974.

Kosut, Hal (ed.). <u>Cyprus 1946-68</u>. New York: Facts on File, 1970.

Labrousse, Alain. <u>The Tupamaros</u>. Harmondsworth: Penguin, 1973.

Laqueur, Walter. <u>Terrorism</u>. Boston:Little Brown, 1977.

Lipset, Seymour Martin. <u>Political Man</u>. Garden City, NY:Doubleday, 1960.

Lodge, Juliet (ed.). <u>Terrorism: A Challenge to the State</u>. New York:St. Martins Press, 1981.

Loizos, Peter. <u>The Greek Gift</u>. New York:St. Martins Press, 1975.

McDonald, Ronald. "Electoral Politics and Uruguayan Political Decay," <u>Inter-American Economics Affairs</u>, 26 (Summer 1972):24-45.

McKeown, Michael. <u>The First Five Hundred</u>. Belfast:Irish News (Pamphlet), 1972.

McStiofain, Sean. <u>Memoirs of a Revolutionary</u>. London:Gordon Cremonesi, 1975.

Maguire, Maria. <u>To Take Arms</u>. London: Macmillan, 1973.

Markides, Kyriacos. <u>The Rise and Fall of the Cyprus Republic</u>. New Haven:Yale University Press, 1977.

Mayans, Ernesto (ed.). <u>Tupamaros</u>. Cuernavaca: Centro Intercultural de Documentation, 1971.

Medhurst, Kenneth. <u>The Basques</u>. London: Minority Rights Group, 1972.

Mercader, Antonio and Vera, Jorge. Tupamaros: estrategia y accion. Montevideo, 1969.

Moss, Robert. Urban Guerrillas. London:Temple Smith, 1972.

National Graves Commission. The Last Post. Dublin, 1976.

Northern Ireland. Department of Finance. Statistics and Economics Unit. Digest of Statistics, Northern Ireland. Belfast, H. M. Stationery Off. (Semi-annual).

Nunez Astrain, Luis. Clases Sociales en Euskadi. San Sebastian: Editorial Txertoa, 1977.

Paget, Julian. Counter-Insurgency Operations. New York:Walker and Company, 1967.

Papachrysostomou, Chr. The Archives of the Fallen. Nicosia:Museum of the National Struggle, 1969.

_____. List of Those Imprisoned. Nicosia:Museum of the National Struggle, 1977.

Pisano, Vittorfranco. Contemporary Italian Terrorism: Analysis and Countermeasures. Washington:Library of Congress, 1979.

Porzecanski, Arturo. Uruguay's Tupamaros. New York:Praeger, 1973.

Ronchey, Alberto. "Guns and Grey Matter," Foreign Affairs, 57 (Spring 1979):921-40.

Rose, Richard. Governing without Consensus. London:Faber and Faber, 1971.

_____. Northern Ireland: Time for Decision. Boston:Beacon Press, 1976.

Rude, George. The Crowd in History: Popular Disturbances in France and England 1730-1848. New York:Wiley, 1964.

121

Russell, Charles. "The Urban Guerrilla in Latin America: A Select Bibliography." Latin American Research Review, 9 (Spring 1974): 37-39.

Silj, Allessandro. Never Again Without a Rifle. New York:Karz, 1979.

Sterling, Claire. The Terror Network. New York:Holt, Rinehart and Winston, 1981.

Stohl, Michael (ed.) The Politics of Terrorism. New York: Dekker, 1979.

Tilly, Charles. The Rebellious Century 1830-1930. Cambridge:Harvard University Press, 1975.

United Nations. Statistical Office. Monthly Bulletin of Statistics. New York.

Uruguay Ministerio del Interior. 7 Meses de Lucha Antisubversion. 1972.

Utley, Thomas. The Lessons of Ulster. London: Dent, 1975.

Wilkinson, Paul. Terrorism and the Liberal State. London:Macmillan, 1977.